"Catherine's ideas always challenge my thinking and push me toward growth."
—**So-Mai Brown,
Licensed Marriage and Family Therapist**

"A reminder that love, acceptance and kindness apply to both the beginning of a relationship as well as long term commitments. This is a book I will revisit many times in the years to come."
—**Bob Alonzi, author of** *I-Stretch & Strengthen:
The Take-Everywhere Exercise System*

"I'm relatively new to my spiritual journey but I found great ease reading *Tantric Mating* … I found it an easy read with some very simple but at the same time deep concepts about relationships and sex that were perfectly explained."
—**Natalie E Barnett, Amazon Reviewer**

Praise for *The Tantric Mastery Series*

"For those readers, men and women, who wish to enrich their love lives, investigating Catherine's sage and well-considered advice could be just the answer and the path you're looking for!"
—*Osho Times*, **international online magazine**

"One of the first things one senses when a word such as "tantric" appears in a title is that the work is fluff. This book is anything but fluff. It is a sensible approach to finding absolute happiness with one's partner ... Worth its weight in gold and should be read over and over. Five stars."
—**Paul A. Broome, author** *Girls Who Don't Believe*

"Full of insights and perspectives that will benefit any relationship and your life in general. The book is enjoyable to read and will deepen all your relationships."
—**Shanti Grace, Chief Administrative Officer, Brain Research Institute, UCLA (retired)**

"I highly recommend Catherine's book to anyone looking for a new strategy on how to have more positive relationships with people, whether that is in the dating world or anywhere else."
—**Nicole Slater, Strategic Marketing and Personal Development Consultant**

"This book is a super-simple, practical and powerful guide to loving well. From listening to your body to talking about anything, this book offers clear action steps to bring more romantic relating into your experience. Use this book to learn what serves life (and juicy connecting). I highly recommend this book!!!"

—**Corey Folsom, Relationship Coach, author of** *Soul Statements*

"Catherine's works are absolutely fundamental, foundational works that EVERY person (single or attached) should read if they're looking to create a happy, fulfilling relationship. *The Tantric Mastery Series* is required reading for all of my clients."

—**Carina Eriksson, Professional Matchmaker**

"Every little chapter is an energy hit for people, period, no matter what your level of experience. Easy to read pithy bites will raise your day to new heights."

—**Ginny Winn, Licensed Marriage and Family Therapist**

The
Tantric Mastery Collection

The Complete Tantric Mastery Series
3-in-1 Compilation

Catherine Auman, LMFT

Green Tara Press

Green Tara Press
Los Angeles, CA
www.greentarapress.com

"The Eyes—Your False Friends," "The Egg Meditation," "Envisioning Your Lover as the God or Goddess They Truly Are," The #1 Thing You Can Do to Improve Your Relationships," "The Quickest Route to Tantric Sex," "Envisioning Your Lover as the God or Goddess They Truly Are,'" and "What Do We Mean by 'Spiritual Relationships'" were previously published in Catherine Auman's book *Shortcuts to Mindfulness: 100 Ways to Personal and Spiritual Growth*.

© 2022 Catherine Auman

All rights reserved. All chapters may be freely copied and shared as long as they are attributed to the author.

Library of Congress In-Publication Data
    Auman, Catherine I.
    Tantric Dating
    1. Self Help 2. Spiritual. 3. Sacred Sexuality

ISBN: 978-1-945085-34-5   Paperback
ISBN: 978-1-945085-34-5   Electronic Book Text

Author Photo by Catherine Auman
Cover Art by Andrea Bogdan
Back Cover Photo by Charity Burnett
Front Cover and Interior Book Design by Lorie DeWorken

CONTENTS

Introduction to *The Tantric Mastery Collection*   xi

TANTRIC DATING

Tantric Dating Introduction   3

Tantric Dating Mindset 11
What Do We Mean by "Tantra?"   13
Tantric Dating vs. Conventional Dating   17
Society Is Against Love   21
The Appearance Issue   25
The Whole Issue of "Chemistry" and "Trusting Your Gut"   29
Is It Really Rejection?   33
What About Toxic People?   37
We're All Spiritual Brothers and Sisters
   Helping Each Other Grow   39
Blaming Other People for Why We're Not Loving   43
It's Up to Me Whether I Love You or Not;
   It's Not Up to You   47
The Invention of Romantic Love   51
The Pain of Romantic Love is Good for You (To a Point)   55
How Do I Open More to Love?   59
Advocating for Love   63

Tantric Dating Exercises 65
EXERCISE #1: The Eyes—Your False Friends   67
EXERCISE #2: The Egg Meditation   71
EXERCISE #3: Tantric Dating Metta   75
EXERCISE #4: Tantric Dating Tonglen   77
EXERCISE #5: Practicing Tantric Dating Principles   79
EXERCISE #6: The Perfect Beloved in This Moment   83

TANTRIC MATING

Tantric Mating Introduction — 89

Tantric Dating Mindset 95

Soulmates Are Created, Romance Is Created — 97

Conventional Expectations — 101

The Work You Do on Your Own — 105

Friendship Is Required for Tantric Sex — 109

Safety Is the Root of Everything — 113

Soulmate Creation and the Centers — 117

Soulmates' Centers Are Aligned — 123

Orgasm Is Not What You Think — 127

Sacred Sexuality — 133

Sex Is a Conversation — 137

Psychedelic Sex — 141

Creating Magic — 145

Building and Maintaining Your Soulmate Status — 151

A Perpetual Honeymoon — 155

Dedicated to Personal and Spiritual Growth — 161

Tantric Mating Exercises 165

EXERCISE #1: Challenging the Conventional Mindset — 167

EXERCISE #2: Are You Soulmate Material? — 171

EXERCISE #3: The #1 Thing You Can Do to Improve Your Relationships — 175

EXERCISE #4: Raise Your Frequency by Working on Your Centers — 179

EXERCISE #5: Atisha Heart Meditation — 181

EXERCISE #6: The Quickest Route to Tantric Sex — 183

TANTRIC RELATING

Tantric Relating INTRODUCTION   189

Tantric Relating Mindset 195

To Tell the Truth or Not, That Is the Question   197
Permission to Be Unkind   201
Don't Rock the Boat, Baby   205
The Spiritual Path of Relating   209
Relating Through the Body   213
Agreements to Talk about Everything   217
The Process of Clearing   221
Clearing the Past   225
Thank You for Bringing That Up   229
Really, Until It's Done   233
Space to Be Upset   237
Praise, Thanks, and Flirting   241
When in Doubt, Touch   247
Relating Romantically   251
The Sky's the Limit   255

Tantric Relating Exercises. 259

EXERCISE #1: Envisioning Your Lover
   as the God or Goddess They Truly Are   261
EXERCISE #2: Do You Want to Tell the Truth?   265
EXERCISE #3: Making Agreements   267
EXERCISE #4: Clean Sweep   269
EXERCISE #5: Raise the Bar   273
EXERCISE #6: What Do We Mean
   by "Spiritual Relationships?"   275

Acknowledgments	279
About the Author	281
Connect with Catherine Auman	283
Works by Catherine Auman	284

Introduction to
The Tantric Mastery Collection

The great avatars of Love who have walked this planet—the Virgin of Guadalupe, Dr. Martin Luther King, Jr., Jesus, and Mr. Rogers to name a few—have blessed us with an incandescent outflowing of love that teaches us by example that there is no end to how loving we can become, and if there is, it's a goal worth aspiring to. It is indeed a lifetime pursuit to develop ourselves as Lovers.

Some people imagine that being kind to strangers is in some way different than the love we share with a partner, but it is the same Love. The more loving you become as an individual, the more love will be reflected back in your life and your partnership(s). The frequency of love is a high vibration, and it can be reached by diligent work on your personal and spiritual growth.

For me, the search to find my Perfect Beloved has been part of my spiritual path. I didn't always see it that way because patriarchal religion taught me not to—that true spiritualty consists of men sitting alone in caves meditating. I felt the shame projected by mainstream culture that looking for and being obsessed with love was "lesser," relegated to denigrated areas of life such as the Women's Section of the newspaper, romance novels, and Hallmark Movies-of-the-Week. Real women (people) (even harder for men walking this path, I suppose) focus on their careers and their friends, and if love finds you, fine, but if you talk about your yearning, it is seen as pathetic and less-than. Romantic love should "just happen," and if it doesn't, you are flawed, and so what? Be happy because single life is awesome.

Later, I was told by the conventional culture that I was "too old" to find love. Then there is the school of thought that if you are truly "feminine," you should sit and passively wait, because men are the only ones who get to choose or pursue who they want. This is obviously a strategy invented by unattractive, undesirable men in order to be able to procure women. Let's not forget the utter fallacy that men are not attracted to powerful women, so as women we should hide our strength and pretend to be dumb in order to find love. All of these lies need to be seen for what they are and rigorously discarded if we are to become free.

When tantra made its surprising appearance in my life, I was exposed to a whole new (to me) worldview that sex, love and romance are sacred. It was an immediate "aha" moment. Learning more about it, I discovered ancient cultures whose origin tales taught that the world is born of sex, such as the conjugal union of Shiva and Shakti. I uncovered religions where God is referred to as "The Beloved" (Sufism), and learned that in tantric relationships the divine is experienced in our partner and in ourselves.

I came to acknowledge that the search for the Beloved is a spiritual path, and I shared my findings in the first book in the series, *Tantric Dating*. The conventional dating world was so cold and unloving that I was determined to learn how to date/search for my beloved by bringing love and awareness to the dating process. That book, much to my surprise, was named one of the Best Dating Books of All Time by BookAuthority. I began offering live *Tantric Dating* workshops in Los Angeles which are consistently well-attended to this day, with participants sharing that the experience is "life-changing."

People kept asking for more so I designed the *Tantric Mastery Series*. The second book, *Tantric Mating*, teaches how to use tantric secrets to create a relationship full of sex, love and romance. These two books became and remain Amazon bestsellers in several categories: Sacred Sexuality, Mate Seeking, and New Age. I am happy that my work is resonating with many readers.

The third book in the series, *Tantric Relating,* is relationship advice to find and keep sex, love and romance. Deceptively simple, these techniques, if implemented, will change your life and your relationships, not just your romantic one(s).

I hope the compilation of these three books into one volume will be helpful for those of you who are new to the work, or for those who'd prefer all the information in one place. I believe the search for love is a noble and elevated spiritual path, not to be relegated as "lesser" than traditionally male pursuits such as careers and building things. You can acknowledge it as honorable in yourself as well, that the search for perfect love and sacred sexuality is a timeless human tradition of which you are a part.

Don't let anyone tell you it's impossible. No matter your age, gender, sexual orientation, body shape, or past trauma, perfect love is available for you. I know it is within your reach to create the sex, love and romance of your dreams, because my life is living proof of it. Here's how.

In love and service,
Catherine Auman LMFT

Tantric Dating

**Bringing Love and Awareness
to the Dating Process**

Tantric Dating
INTRODUCTION

It was a major birthday—one of those years when you take stock of if you're where you want to be. In most areas of life, I had to admit I was doing great: successful in my chosen career, great health, lovely friends, a cute apartment, financially stable—most of the things that everyone wants—except for the only thing that had ever really mattered—being in a soulmate relationship with my Perfect Beloved.

Not that I hadn't tried. Ever since I first discovered boys (outside my brother) in kindergarten, I'd been trying. After countless blind dates, bad dates and bad boys, relationship advice books and columns, online and in-person dating, an early foray (a bit unwillingly) into "free love" culture, endless hours of therapy, many, many relationships and two failed marriages, I had to admit: I was a Dating Disaster.

I recounted all this to a long-time friend in the Bay Area who asked how she could support me. Since she was actively involved in online dating, I suggested we cheerlead each other a couple times a week. We began chatting frequently late at night, reviewing dates and deciphering texts. Then she promptly met someone and with that, I was alone again.

I made the decision to go for it. Really go for it this time, no matter what. I was going to get to the bottom of this and become a Master of Dating and Relationships. I decided to hack dating once and for all, whatever it took. And for me, it took a lot.

Sitting on my couch on Saturday nights, watching Netflix while sipping a glass of wine wasn't working. I needed to get into action. I joined five online dating sites and over twenty Meetups (which is great because you are always getting invitations in your inbox). I downloaded an app which had a calendar of all the art openings in town and ventured out to art gallery openings (free wine and intriguing hipsters). I went back to therapy to complete some still-unfinished business from childhood (I had been in therapy a lot, but still … sometimes when you come from a difficult childhood it takes a while), and hired a coach. An unusual dating coach—I hired a Pickup Artist.

I had read *The Game* back in the 00s and realized those guys know a lot that is not taught in "girl game" (dating) books which overall are pretty lame. I'd always been a bit shy and afraid to go up and speak to a man I found attractive, and pickup coaching got me over all that.

With the help of my coach I began going out "in the field," meaning into real life where men might be hanging out. I went to anything I could think of to meet men, mostly dead ends. Little by little my dating skills improved, and the men I was attracting grew closer and closer to my heart's longing. Dating actually became fun, and I played in the field enjoying my new freedom.

I went on over 150 online first dates, followed by second and third dates, and sometimes it seemed to be working out. I met 2-3 men a week, sometimes 2-3 in a day. I made myself go out: Meetups, gallery openings, singles events, networking events, Green Drinks, poetry readings, museum outings, and basically every time I went to Trader Joe's. I traveled with wing-girls and without and challenged myself to approach men I found interesting. I created little games for when I was discouraged (which was often), such as before I went to sleep, I needed to contact 10 guys online. Usually 2 would get back. I made progress in therapy, and worked hard with my coach.

One question always nagged me though, how did all of this coexist with my spiritual life?

You see, I'd lived at the Osho ashram in India for a year, a full-time immersion in tantra and meditation. The way potential lovers met there was very different than in the conventional world. People there were friends first, and after that would see if a sexual friendship was possible. In our contemporary dating scene in the West, "the friend zone" is considered death. At the ashram, and in tantra, the Friend Zone is exactly where you want to be. Only if you and your lover are friends will you establish the trust and intimacy necessary for good sex and a good relationship to happen.

In exercises in the tantra groups, we got close to and "fell in love" with people we would never have chosen if we had let our eyes be the primary criteria the way we do in the West. We learned to feel another person's frequency, to assess our level of comfort and safety. We practiced telling the radical truth to each other, a practice frowned on by conventional dating. We enjoyed the process of meeting one another rather than considering it a huge, irritating chore. And we experienced loving who was present in this moment, rather than waiting for one who may never come.

For years, I couldn't reconcile what I'd learned at the ashram with the conventional dating world I was now attempting to navigate. But little by little, I began to put together how dating could be part of the spiritual path. I watched my judgments, my prejudices—did I really believe that only conventionally good-looking people were worthy of love? I observed how I searched for the wrong things instead of the only quality that's really important—kindness.

I came to realize that the reason I had attracted men who were half-loving was because I was half-loving. I painfully accepted that the common denominator in my relationship problems was me. And if I wanted to meet a man who was truly loving, I would have to evolve beyond being unloving toward the men I was meeting or even viewing online.

I had to confront the romantic Disney-esque fantasies that had been fed to me in movies, books, and songs that love would come to me by magic. I had to stand up to the ageism of the culture and inside myself that women (people) of a certain age are too old to find love, or that men only like younger women. This is emphatically not true. After I had made progress in my dating work, I dated men from ages 28 to 68 and everywhere in between. (The 28-year old, a true looker from Turkey, begged me to take him as my boyfriend. I said no.) I had to work hard to overcome all these cultural myths. Because they are myths and because they're commonly held to be true, they are insidious.

Eventually I became more loving through my process of "Tantric Dating," loving enough to attract a loving man. After 3½ years of hard effort, I met my Perfect Beloved. I didn't recognize him at first. It's true he pursued me, but if I hadn't learned what I did through decades of work on myself, we would not met nor have the Perfect Soulmate relationship we have today. We got married after two years of being together, and together have created a relationship where both of us are always saying, "I didn't know a relationship could be this good."

And so, I want to teach you my method of Tantric Dating that attracted and created the relationship I dreamed of since kindergarten. Some people have reported profound shifts in their attitudes after reading this book. Others have criticized it for being a little slim, which it is. I still stand by its content because if you really digest it, it's all you'll need. Please bring the willingness to examine the brainwashing of the conventional world and decide for yourself. Choose to become the loving person that your heart knows you are. Share it with the world, and Love cannot deny you.

TANTRIC DATING MINDSET

What Do We Mean by "Tantra?"

When most people hear the word "tantra" they think of sex, and often here in the Western world you'll see "tantra" used as a marketing term such as come to this or buy this because it's TANTRA, you've seen this right? Actually, Osho, a spiritual teacher and Tantra Master from India, explained it this way: At the essence, all teachings basically boil down to one of two paths to God, enlightenment, realization, whatever term you want to use: the Yogic or the Tantric.

In New Age circles you'll see it all mushed together, but if you look closely, you'll see that there are actually two separate paths. The Yogic path says that there's something you have to do to get to God: you have to eat a certain way, or you have to never be angry, you have to wear a certain kind of clothes, or you should not have sex. There are a myriad of ways you can develop and try to change yourself, and in the West we would say we're very "yogic" because we're all developing ourselves, we want to become better, we want to become superior people, and we want to become high(er).

The Tantric path, which is not as well-known, is that there's nothing to be done, everything is already perfect. In this moment, is anything missing? All is permitted, all is holy, all is divine, there's nothing you need to improve. You don't need to eat a certain way; you don't need to stop being sexual; if you're angry be angry. Osho would have people get totally angry, and in his Dynamic Meditation they'd just go crazy and mad and spill out all their anger instead of trying to repress it. The point was not to create a world full of angry people, the point was to create people who are fully human, and being angry is an essential part of being human. So the tantric path would say that everything about you is human and beautiful including your anger, including your pain, including your sexuality. Osho said celebrate everything you are: this is the tantric path.

There have been different paths calling themselves tantra, and you will find some that actually are yogic in that they teach exercises to become a super lover, a tantra superstar. Osho's Neo-Tantra was not about that; it was facing your fears, growing yourself up about love and sex, and in the process experiencing yourself as a fully sexual being.

Tantric Dating vs. Conventional Dating

Conventional dating in and of itself encourages us to think there's something wrong with other people and something wrong with us. Other people don't look right, and you don't look right. They're not lovable, and you're not lovable. They don't have the cool moves; you don't have the cool moves. The conventional mindset encourages us to see other people and ourselves as weird and unattractive and disposable.

The conventional dating process encourages us to feel I'm not doing it right, I don't meet the right people, I'm not attractive enough to date. For women it's "I'm not pretty enough" and for guys it's "I'm not accomplished enough" continuing the deadly cycle of over-focus on women's appearance and men's financial status. These myths about who's lovable and who isn't actually keep people home and not looking for love because they believe the myth that "I'm not good enough;" "I'm not pretty enough;" "I'm not accomplished enough;" "I'm not hot enough;" it's endless. It's all ego stuff that someone's surface appearance is not to my liking.

Everyone you meet on a date is seen through the frame of whether they are a candidate for the fantasy of perfect love or not. This is very harsh isn't it? If they're not a candidate, get rid of them quickly followed by an amusing story for friends: "God I couldn't stand being on that date for so long; it was so awful… etc." This whole conventional mindset is anti-love, whether love for self or others.

From a tantric perspective every single person you meet is the right person in this moment. If you look at the person next to you, in this moment this is your beloved. She or he is your true love, right here, right now. The beloved is not somebody you're going to meet in the future; it's not somebody who's going to ride in on a white horse or be spotted across the dance floor. Right now, this is where love is available; this is who it is possible to love. Are you available for this love? If we're always thinking I can't love this other person because they aren't good enough for me that's about you, not the other person. How about: let me enjoy this other spiritual being and even if it's not the romantic fantasy, we are in this perfect spot together sharing love in this perfect moment.

Society Is Against Love

Society is designed to lure you away from being intimate with others because you are not spending any money during this time. Intimacy is the enemy of consumerism because your sense of well-being is so greatly enhanced that you do not need to buy material goods to be happy. —Peter Rengel

I first met Peter Rengel as one of the facilitators of the Love, Intimacy and Sexuality workshops at the Human Awareness Institute (HAI). They're located in the Bay Area, and I learned a great deal while moving up to Level Five in their system. I also worked individually with Peter as my therapist, so I was lucky enough to learn a lot from this man whose life mission is "to help people love themselves more." How awesome is that?

Peter pointed out, as in the quote above, that society is designed to seduce you away from being intimate with others because you won't spend money if you're in love and satisfied. If you're in love and fulfilled, what do you need to buy?

I checked this out with a friend of mine who's been married for 25 years. He said oh yeah, he and his wife just work, stay in and cook, watch movies and make love, and that's about all they do. They are very happy with their lives.

Think how much money is spent in the dating process; it's a whole industry. You have to spend money on your dates, buy expensive food, and drink more alcohol than you usually drink. You have to buy dating clothes, which for women must be sexy. Guys have to show off how much money they make. Certain restaurants position themselves as dating hot spots as well as certain hip bars, and there are pricey singles' events and online dating sites to join. It's a multi-million dollar business to keep you single and unhappy because if you fall in love and fall out of all that and therefore aren't spending any money, society will stop. So the whole shebang is anti-love, as Peter pointed out, which is really mind boggling.

You'll also notice it's no accident that the conventional dating mindset is the consumer model in which you are looking to acquire a high-value item, and then when that one is used up you purchase another that is presumably more "expensive."

The Appearance Issue

For many people the biggest barrier to finding a partner is the appearance of the other person. It's hard to live in this culture and not be brainwashed to believe that only certain people are attractive. In the mainstream mindset, only conventionally good-looking people get to be considered sexually appealing and therefore worthy of love.

I was lucky enough to have this pseudo-reality shattered in tantra groups and later on at HAI. The first method used to challenge us was having us be naked all the time. It's difficult at first, but you get used to being around what people really look like which is quite different of course than the photoshopped images we are taught to lust after. It's a good practice to get comfortable being naked with other people (which you can do at spas or clothing-optional resorts)—you get to witness everyone's vulnerable humanity.

What took it to another level of awareness for me, though, was the exercises we did naked and blindfolded where we would reach out and touch and stroke each other—maybe an arm, someone's precious heart—and we would sense without being able to see: what is the nature of my attraction to this person? What kind of energy do the two of us have without the prejudice of sight? We would move on to touch somebody else asking ourselves, what is the actual nature of my attraction with this body? Is it a friendship? A sexual connection? A combination of that? Is it repellent because it reminds me of my parents? Or a soft, being, togetherness?

Not being able to see honed my ability to sense the differences in energies and the truth of my attraction. Those of us in the group found that we were attracted to people we never would have imagined, and we all fell in love with each other no matter what we looked like.

Looks are one thing we can't control, along with age and bone structure. For me it's actually become one of the least interesting things about a person, because it's what people are born with and can't control. I would much prefer to feel the actual nature of my attraction to a person versus what I've been conditioned to desire. We've been conditioned to eat junk food; we've been conditioned to want many things that are "toxic." It's the ego clinging to the idea that I, the great I, must have a person on my arm who makes me look even better.

The Whole Issue of "Chemistry" and "Trusting Your Gut"

In the dating world, most everyone nods and agrees when people say that what they're looking for is "chemistry." Other similar phrases you'll hear are "using their intuition" and "trusting their gut." These are often the same people who believe they can tell within five seconds whether or not someone is worthy of their love.

I'd like to address that as a therapist. An article in my book, *Shortcuts to Mindfulness: 100 Ways to Personal and Spiritual Growth* entitled "Your Worst Nightmare" cites Terry Gorski, a renowned chemical dependency counselor. Gorski states that when you have the feeling of love at first sight, you should turn around and run in the opposite direction. Sometimes what we think of as "chemistry" means programming from our childhood, and it may not be a good sign.

As an extreme example, we've all heard of a woman beaten by her father in childhood, who now doesn't leave relationships where the man beats her up. We wonder, why doesn't she leave? Well, she was programmed in childhood that love equals getting beat up, so she's going to feel "chemistry" when she meets a guy who carries that energy. At first he's going to seem like a gentleman, and she's going to think, "Oh, finally I met somebody who isn't an abuser," but that "chemistry" that comes from wiring in childhood is going to prevail most of the time unless she's done work to disempower it.

So when people say they're looking for "chemistry" often they are looking at issues that are going to trigger unfinished business from the past. Hopefully that will entice the person to get into therapy and stop being attracted to someone who hurts them or is in some other way unkind or not good for them.

Also often what we call "chemistry" is that the other person is close to the cultural ideal. The more someone looks like Brad Pitt or Sophia Vergara, the more people are going to believe they feel "chemistry." Check it out: oh my God I finally met Brad Pitt—he's rich and handsome and famous. That's "chemistry."

Or people who are verbally acute, are very good at speaking and have excellent social skills, often times it seems as though we have chemistry with them. Well, guess what, they have chemistry with everyone; it's not special with you.

So "gut instinct" or intuition: I'm not saying there's never a benefit to intuition but it's often unreliable. It's based on either some kind of childhood stuff that's still being worked through or what society tells you you should want. It could be a past life connection, and the two of you have been past life lovers for a millennium, but you're not supposed to be together in this lifetime. Intuition can be helpful, but intuition alone is not the most reliable compass.

There are many things that can trigger a strong reaction to meeting a new person. It's possible the feeling is a good sign, but I'm suggesting that people not blindly go "Oh, it's chemistry." When you have that feeling, realize there could be many possibilities and don't just blindly believe it means this is "The One."

Is It Really Rejection?

Sophisticated conventional daters will sooner or later come across the mindset that "dating is a series of rejections" and that to be successful dater, it's about becoming okay with the inevitable. One aphorism you'll hear is "If you want to get more comfortable with rejection, go out and get rejected five times"—the idea being that you will learn to stop taking it so personally. In a way, I applaud these efforts as a step on the way to realizing that dating doesn't have to hurt so much, having gone through a similar process earlier myself. I remember a time when I was afraid to date because it seemed so awful to have to reject people, and I often hear women saying the same thing. Having to reject can be almost as painful as being the rejected one.

Some conventional daters use a phrase they've learned in 12-step programs that "Rejection is God's protection," helping them see that perhaps this was not the right person or the right time and that maybe the "rejection" happened for a good reason.

But what happens to us when we use this word "rejection?" What does "rejection" feel like? Terrible, bad, and humiliating. It also feels horrible and cruel to "reject" another human being. We must be careful in the way we choose our words—they can create all kinds of states, situations, and mindsets, and the word "rejection" can create incapacitating feelings.

What if we do away altogether with this concept of "rejection?" Instead, we could see dating situations as we do with potential friends: you meet someone at an event and hang out; you have a good time talking, but you aren't necessarily moved to make plans to see them again. In dating, this would be called "rejection," but in ordinary life there's no rejecting going on, you just aren't going to hang out. In dating this scenario is experienced as painful, and it doesn't have to be any more so than it is meeting someone at a networking event.

What if we said instead "it's just not a good fit" or "s/he wasn't my cup of tea," or "seemed like a lovely person, but there must have been things I wasn't seeing about him/her." How about if we say if we're "ghosted:" "My goodness, that's a person who doesn't seem to communicate very well, because they seemed like they did but then suddenly they dropped off the planet. I need to be with a better communicator."

In using words the conventional dating mindset encourages us to use we may become tougher, steeling ourselves against "rejection." The whole concept of "rejecting" comes from the ego: this person is not good enough for me, or I am not good enough for them. What if we just enjoy our precious time with this person, and if it's not right to be with them again, it doesn't have to hurt us. It could be held in a loving way that's neither rejecting people nor being rejected by them.

What About Toxic People?

I know it's quite popular, but I don't agree with this concept that certain people are toxic. It doesn't make any sense to me at all to label people that way; I find it harsh and inaccurate. Perhaps it might be helpful to label some behaviors that people do as "toxic" so that we learn to develop strong boundaries, but the appointing of some beings as "toxic" is often used as a justification not to love people.

In a tantric perspective nothing is toxic; in a yogic perspective everything is either toxic or non-toxic. In the tantric worldview nothing is forbidden; everything is holy. Therefore, a challenging relationship with a difficult person may be just what we need to make us aware of where and how we need to grow.

Observe it: your mind is busy coming up with reasons why not to love people. They're toxic, or not good-looking enough, or not spiritual, or they have too many problems. Where are these people who have no problems? People come with problems, and they're going to stir you and make your life difficult, and that's a good thing.

This idea of "people who are toxic" could be a pretext for "how do I keep people away?" Not consciously, of course, it's subtle. Who can I keep away from me because they're too toxic, and they'll bring me problems? All of these people that I don't want to let close. Really, that's focusing on how to keep love away.

I'm asking you to flip your question 180 degrees to: How can I allow people to come close? Use your intelligence to figure out how to let people in instead of how to keep people out. Who are you going to allow yourself to love? Consider that instead of thinking about what and who is toxic. Open up and let us in.

We're All Spiritual Brothers and Sisters Helping Each Other Grow

An attitude I developed while hanging out at the Ashram and basking in the tantric atmosphere was *we're all spiritual brothers and sisters helping each other grow*. I'd never thought of the men I was involved with this way, so it was revolutionary, and I'd never been in an environment where men and women treated each other as such. It was beautiful and loving in stark contrast to conventional dating where everyone considers others as either a candidate for the Perfect Love or the garbage can.

A brother of mine on the planet, a spiritual brother or sister who's also evolving—I believe that everyone's evolving even if they don't use that language. We come together for these romantic and sexual encounters to evolve in a certain way together. We don't know for how long; we're not in charge of that part, I don't think. So it's been a helpful mindset for me to hold that we're helping each other grow, rather than clinging to a fantasy outcome that might or might not be for our higher good.

The fairy-tale fantasy is that a man is going to come fully formed as the Perfect Prince, or for guys, that the Dream Woman is going to come as this totally voluptuous, always wanting to have sex, always loving person. If the Prince was always ready for sex that would be fine too, but it's this idea that these perfect lovers are going to come to us fully formed that's the cause of a lot of problems. Who's fully formed? Only a person who's not human or who's stopped growing, so when you meet a real person and they're not fully formed, you're going to be disappointed if you're immersed in the conventional mindset.

But if you're holding it that we're all evolving and growing and we're spiritual brothers and sisters, you can allow the other person to relax in your tender and warm presence and evolve along with you. Both men and women have difficult things to overcome as we are learning to become more loving, and this path of dating, relationships, and sexuality can be one of the roadways to God. It can rapidly accelerate your growth and lead you further along the path to becoming an ultimately loving person.

Blaming Other People for Why We're Not Loving

When we explain that the reason we don't have love in our lives is that we can't find the right person, or that other people are flawed or wrong in some way, it's putting the blame outside ourselves for why we don't have love, versus I'm not living in love because I'm not loving. The truth is: I'm not loving to the people I meet, I reject them, and I don't make time for them.

Some of the ancient *tantrikas* (people who practice tantra) were tortured for their beliefs because people were so prejudiced against them. In one sect, the couple lived their entire lives sewn together into one garment. Now think about it, in today's world you can barely stand to have your lover over for an hour and a half before you start bumping against something vaguely irritating.

Of course I'm exaggerating (am I?) but we've all gotten used to having things our own way, and our egos clash when we spend much time together. In one of the exercises at the ashram, we experimented with a partner where we didn't let go of their hand for three hours. We would walk around doing every minute thing together, and I saw how much time it takes to be intimate. It took so long to just reach out and get food in the food line, to walk over to the table together—it was exquisite and, you know, a real luxury. I really got the sense that it takes so much time to be loving, and we just don't have or make that time. Everyone's too busy.

If you want to sit and have a coffee date with someone and you want to enjoy them no matter what they're like, you're going to have to relax and have it take time instead of be wondering how quickly you can leave. It's going to take time to figure out how to savor the person. It's going to take time to have love, and it's going to take time to turn yourself into a loving person.

I hear this a lot: I can't find anybody; there's nobody to love. Really? There are 10 million people in greater LA, 20 million in Southern California—how could you possibly not find someone? That's about you, that's about me, that's about us if we can't find someone; it's not about the lack of other candidates. If we're willing to take spiritual responsibility, it's not the other person's fault. The other person is an opportunity for us to learn to become more loving, and who does that need to be? That could be anyone—it could be that homeless person sitting on the bench, but we make it so hard.

It's Up to Me Whether I Love You or Not; It's Not Up to You

It's all up to me if I love you or not; it's not up to you. It actually has nothing to do with you whatsoever. It has everything to do with whether my heart's open to love or not. So when I'm sitting across from you at a date and we're meeting for the first time or the tenth time, it's not about whatever characteristics and traits you may or may not have. I decide to love or not love. Not you.

It's a great spiritual exercise to sit and watch your ego try to convince you why it's not possible to love this person. Your ego will whisper, "Well, she's wearing a sweater like that—I can't love a person who wears that brand." That's me and not the sweater-wearer, right? The type of clothing she's wearing and whether that makes her loveable to me has nothing to do with her—it has to do with my prejudices. You can also use this exercise if you're brave enough to show you how unloving you are, because your fantasy is that you're this great loving person, and you can't even love a simple being who's sitting across from you.

Watching oneself this way on dates can be used as a spiritual discipline to see "what in me is in the way of love," because if I'm not meeting anybody through the dating process, it's about me not the supposedly-deficient other people. Osho once said, "If you are alone and lonely it's because there are too many conditions on your love."

We can develop within ourselves a tantric approach that there are many ways to love "you," the "you" who is in front of me in this moment. In this moment I really can't think of any reason why not to love you. I don't know how long we're going to know each other— maybe for twenty more minutes and maybe two years and maybe the rest of our lives, but right now in this moment it's up to me, so I choose love.

The Invention of Romantic Love

I read a fascinating book in college called *Love in the Western World* that said that romantic love was invented in the 1200s by the Troubadours. You remember the Troubadours, wearing those sexy little puff pants, walking around playing lutes, singing about their ladylove. They would elevate a woman onto a pedestal and long ceaselessly for her; the whole point of chivalrous love was that it was never consummated. It was a sexist day and age, so it was all about men adoring a woman, and the point was to idealize the beloved but never come down to earth for love's trials and tribulations.

What's really fascinating, even more than the fact that romantic love didn't exist before that time, was that the people who inspired it, the Cathars, were actually singing to God, not a woman. They were an ecstatic *bhakti* sort of cult, singing hymns to God in an almost sexual frenzy. They were persecuted for their beliefs and mode of worship (they were later burned alive) so they hid their passion by pretending their songs were about a woman instead of God.

So the whole notion of romantic love was a lie. It was a cover up for a yearning that is spiritual, not a desire for a human person. It was created to point towards something that's actually not achievable on the physical plane. Romantic love wasn't intended to result in what we would today consider a relationship. Instead it was about pining—the essence of romantic love is that you're in pain longing for a perfect person who doesn't exist and you can't have.

We celebrate romantic love; we want romantic love; I personally love the fantasy of romantic love. Everybody has had moments of perfect romantic love, right? And how long did they last? Hours, days, you can do it for years if the person is not available. If the person has rejected you, you can fantasize about them for decades. It was never meant to be anything tangible, or of the real world.

Osho once said that all your romantic love affairs will be thwarted so that you'll keep searching for what you're really seeking: Divine Love.

The Pain of Romantic Love is Good for You (To a Point)

Romantic love, as we said, as invented by the Troubadours, is a spiritual longing for what cannot be had here on the earth plane. The object of romantic love is not really a human being, it's an idealized image, perhaps a fragmented memory of a person we once knew. Romantic love actually prefers to be unrequited; causing a desire for someone you can't have that's so bad you want to tear your heart out. You elevate the other onto a pedestal above you, and thus you are of lesser value. To really make it passionate, it helps to have been rejected. If you imagine it was because you are not good enough or deficient in some way, well, that leads to some really delicious self-flagellation.

Could there be a spiritual purpose for this? How could it be good for us? I think it's explained by this Kahlil Gibran quote, "Your pain is the breaking of the shell that encloses your understanding." This has helped me understand why I've had pain; why my patients have pain, and why the human race suffers so much: because when we are in pain it breaks our hearts and that gives us an opportunity for understanding. We can begin to develop compassion for our own suffering and the suffering of others. Then Love starts becoming available, not as a fantasy "my lover looks like Brad Pitt" or some dream girl, but because I'm becoming a loving person to my neighbors, friends, family, and loved ones. I can start looking for someone who will love me back instead of rejecting me and finding me unworthy, leaving me feeling like pond scum.

A tantra teacher I met the other day said to me, "The heart that breaks is not the True Heart." Wow! The True Heart isn't the egoic heart. Our limited little hearts break because we were looking for the wrong thing. We were looking for the fantasy Brad Pitt who is wealthy and fit and always does the right romantic things and drives such-and-such car and is my armpiece, impressing my friends. My ego can get all puffed up that I'm this great lover, when actually I'm not very loving at all because what I'm seeking is something to enhance my ego. That's what gets broken so we can actually become lovers.

The egoic mindset is, in order for me to be loving, the other person has to be what my ego wants them to be. I will only be loving if the other person is cool enough for me. I will only be loving if the other person is conventionally beautiful, or isn't of a different body size, or isn't an Arab or Muslim or Syrian or Jew or black or white, etc.— that's the only way I'll be loving. That's what's going on the planet: You have to be a certain way for me to love you.

How Do I Open More to Love?

The question comes up: "How do I open more to love?" If I'm working on myself to become a more loving person, and seeking increased emotional and sexual pleasure, how do I go about it?

I would offer you a beautiful, mind-blowing perspective from one of my teachers, Radha Luglio, who has a large tantra practice in Italy. When asked this question she answered: it's not a question of how do I open more, it's a question of where am I holding.

Wow. In this moment, if I pay attention, I can tell where I'm holding. And I've yet to meet a person who when asked where they're holding, isn't able to identify it immediately. Is it a tightness in the belly, the throat? Is there a restriction around the heart, the breath, the genitals? Is it a stuckness from a previous relationship that needs to be cleared? Perhaps a hardness around the heart, or a wish to slow down.

It's right here in the present moment. We can go in and do some deep work in psychotherapy which definitely helps, but in this moment where am I holding against love? You can ask this while in the moment with these people right now; you can ask it on a dinner date. My emotions seem to be freezing up; does this remind me of my mother? Or I don't like people like this, or am I just scared?

You can scan yourself while making love: where am I holding, where am I tensing up? How am I guarding myself against love in this moment? What am I telling myself; what is my mind saying? A lot of times when we're making love we get scared to go a little further, right? It's frightening to get more intimate, but that's about me; it's not the other person's fault. I'm not more loving because he's not making love right—we may try to make it their fault unless we can be strong and truthful and ask ourselves, how am I holding back at this moment from love and pleasure?

We're always trying to blame someone outside ourselves as to why we're not loving. It helps to actually go into the body and feel where the holding pattern is, and identify it. Awareness changes things. The very fact that you have taken responsibility for your own love and pleasure rather than blaming someone or something outside yourself changes the whole experience. Then you can breathe more fully into the present moment, face your fears, communicate, and expand into areas of yet-unknown bliss.

Advocating for Love

So what we are advocating is taking a look at how the conventional view of love actually destroys love, and then making the efforts necessary to turn ourselves into lovers, that is, truly loving people. Making a decision to go against the conventional worldview of daters-as-consumers deciding which shiny new object to purchase. Choosing against being people whose minds instead of hearts run the show, analyzing who is or is not worthy of love based on a set of prejudices as insidious as racism or religious intolerance.

In the world today we have a hate problem; and according to the World Health Organization, we have a growing loneliness and isolation problem which is as detrimental to health as smoking and heart disease. There are a lot of single people sitting in their homes feeling hopeless and lonely—they can't find love in a city of ten million people. It doesn't make sense. The problem is not that there's no one out there to love. The problem is that we're not loving enough to be able to see the abundance of potential lovers.

One way it makes sense is if I work on myself to become a loving person, I'll have ten million lovers. If there's ten million persons in the city, I have potentially ten million lovers—that's kind of sexy, isn't it?

When we are overflowing with love we love everything. You know those moments you've had when you love everything and everyone? Those times often don't last very long, but by working on yourself you can maintain them for longer and longer periods. Every person and every thing seems right to you—that's when you are truly a lover.

How much of a loving person am I? That's really the question.

TANTRIC DATING EXERCISES

EXERCISE #1:
The Eyes—Your False Friends

I often send my single patients to Starbucks to sit and people watch, in a different way than they are used to. I ask them to scan for people who look kind, responsible, trustworthy: the type of person, for example, who thinks it would be fun to coach Little League after work. People often get all tangled up in their love lives because the kind of person who would make a good parent to their future kids does not look like the person who fuels their erotic fantasies.

Back when I was studying tantra in India, we did many of our exercises blindfolded. When we couldn't see, we learned to read the information our bodies were giving us about a person, such as whether or not they could be trusted, whether or not their energy was compatible with ours.

Experimenting in such an environment of trust and vulnerability, we all fell in love with each other regardless of who our eyes might have pre-judged as unworthy.

It seems to me that the way the advertising industry spends billions to convince us that only people who look a certain way are desirable may be related to alarming new statistics about a 60% increase in reports of chronic and crippling loneliness. We are endlessly encouraged to focus on abs and sexiness, not on whether a person would make a good friend or partner. Some of the images selling perfume are down right frightening—if you look closely enough, several of the male models, although conventionally good looking, have the menacing stare of a rapist.

The reports back from Starbucks are that this practice is revolutionary. For many of the clients who come to me lonely and wishing they were partnered, their eyes have become their false friends, encouraging them to search in a way that can't bring them happiness. Osho, the great tantra master, once said, "If you are alone and lonely, it is only because you have too many criteria on your love."

Even if you're not concerned with dating or finding a partner, consider how relying primarily on your eyes for information might be keeping you from more fully exploring smell, touch, sound, and taste. Closing your eyes, getting out of the realm of the visual, is one of the most transformative practices you could take up. In the same way that silence can be the most beautiful sound of all, not seeing in the way you've been trained to see could offer you unexpected vision.

EXERCISE #2:
The Egg Meditation

I invented The Egg Meditation after reading *Becoming a Woman* by Dr. Toni Grant. The book was the first time I encountered the idea that as women, we are losing our yin. Dr. Grant never used that language, but as a Jungian she taught that humans are made up of different components or subpersonalities, and that as modern women; we are emphasizing our active "doing" parts at the expense of our quiet "being" parts. Today, women are busy expressing our assertiveness: becoming CEO's, stripping for our lovers and being on top. We reject what has classically been considered female: being quiet, receptive, and demure. We're all yang and no yin.

When I took sex education in high school, we were shown the most amazing video of an egg being impregnated by a sperm. There She sat, unmoving, glowing, queenly, radiating, waiting patiently in all her splendor. The sperm were wriggling and squirming and jockeying for position, all of them anxious to enter Her. One victorious little tadpole finally succeeded. The egg didn't move a muscle, and, except for a little squeal of ecstasy when he entered, appeared unmoved by the whole experience.

The old fashioned way of pursuit was reportedly like this: men pursued women who were non-active. Men did all the work. Then during the radical changes of the 70's, Germaine Greer exhorted women to take the lead and pursue whichever men we wanted—it seemed like a good idea at the time. Men and women should certainly do whatever is right for their personal temperament. Nevertheless, neither modern men nor women have any connection to their yin self.

I took some time and meditated on the Egg, imagining myself as Her: sitting silently, radiating, waiting. After practicing a few times, I took it on the road. Since I'm an average looking woman, I'd never been approached all that much in bars, so as usual, I sat and watched all the hotties move on each other. I closed my eyes there on my barstool and did my Egg Meditation, envisioning myself as the Queen Egg, glowing, unmoving, and calm. When I opened my eyes, much to my surprise, several attractive men had wriggled up, jockeying for position. I never got approached so much in all my life as I did that night.

Yang is looking for yin, sorely missing in today's world. I'm not advocating that women give up the gains we've made, not by a long shot. But both men and women are missing the element of yin. That's why some men think they want younger or submissive women. Most modern men don't really want submissive; they want a worthy partner. But yang is looking for yin and not more yang. There has to be a balance.

So just for a few minutes, imagine…you're the queen Egg, sitting unmoving… getting fully in touch with your feminine side.

EXERCISE #3:
Tantric Dating Metta

Metta is a Sanskrit word for friendliness, good will, loving kindness. As a practice it has many forms, many translations. Here is a simple one for you to use to develop and expand your love and kindness toward others:

Lie or sit comfortably with eyes closed. (This prayer can also be said anywhere or anytime as a stealth move, and no one needs to know.) Begin to breathe and repeat the following prayer:

May I be happy.

May I be peaceful

May I be safe.

May I awaken to my true nature.

May I be free.

Think of someone who needs this prayer, someone whom it seems has wronged you, or someone you have trouble loving:

May you be happy.

May you be peaceful

May you be safe.

May you awaken to your true nature.

May you be free.

Then visualize all of us in the world, together:

May all beings be happy.

May all beings be peaceful

May all beings be safe.

May all beings awaken to their true nature.

May all beings be free.

EXERCISE #4:
Tantric Dating Tonglen

Tonglen is a Tibetan Buddhist practice for developing compassion by giving and receiving. The purpose is to reduce selfishness, purify karma, and to develop and expand loving kindness. The Dalai Lama is said to practice t*onglen* daily, and Pema Chodron has written and talked about it.

Start by sitting or lying quietly, and begin to observe the breath. On the next inhale, imagine breathing in the pain of other people, people whose pain is very real to you in some way. This could be an individual you know, one you know of, or a group of people such as refugees or schoolchildren or your family. Breathe in with the longing to relieve their suffering

Then, when you exhale, send out with your breath to that person or group, comfort and happiness, love and joy. Repeat the inhale and exhale, giving and receiving, until you feel your own heart expanding with love.

Being Tantric Daters, we might imagine breathing in the pain and suffering of all the single people who don't have enough love in their lives, and sending out love and joy and happiness to all.

Osho once said there is nothing wrong with anybody except they didn't get enough love. Let's try in our own small way to rectify that situation.

EXERCISE #5: Practicing Tantric Dating Principles

To put Tantric Dating principles into practice, it's helpful to examine more closely what might be holding us back from love. Using a journal or just sitting quietly, meditate on these questions:

1. We've been brainwashed into accepting a list of conventional search criteria based on looks, age, financial status, body size, and other unloving prejudices. From a tantric mindset, we might prefer to create a list of loving criteria to guide us. Examples might be: compassionate, kind, shows up in service to others, does some kind of volunteer work, is on a personal growth path. List your original criteria and your new. Which list is more likely to create love in your life?

2. Consider a time when "chemistry" steered you wrong. What did you learn from this?

3. Recall a time or a relationship in which you felt rejected, or when you felt you had to reject someone. Is there a way you could reframe that story so nobody, including yourself, got hurt?

4. If I live in a world in which everyone is evolving, and we're spiritual brothers and sisters helping each other grow, how does that change my mindset when I'm dating? Can I allow other people to be clumsily looking for love, just like I am?

5. We are all a mixture of yin and yang qualities. Previously it was considered right that men should be yang and women yin, but few of us want to live in that kind of world anymore. What are your yang strengths? How about your yin? What yin qualities have you, perhaps, because we still live in a primarily

patriarchal world, judged harshly in yourself or others?

6. Sit, relax, and breathe, and turn your attention inward. Where are you holding tension right now? Without trying to change it, notice and be- come aware—is there often tension in this place? Is it chronic, or just of this moment? Does the attention and breath soften it at all? How is this interfering with being able to experience more pleasure? Exhale and let go...

7. How could I be a more loving person?

EXERCISE #6:
The Perfect Beloved in This Moment

You've heard it many times: truth is in the present moment. The past is made up of memories which are not always accurate as you may have experienced, and the future hasn't happened yet so is all conjecture. Sandwiched in between stands the present moment as the only reality.

I had an overwhelming experience of this sitting quietly at the Burning Ghats, the place where Indians burn their dead. I liked to go sit there and gaze out at the river with the cows, cowherds, and women washing colorful fabrics on the banks. The sun was shining overhead with only a few clouds, the sounds of life murmuring far away from this temple of death, the air rich and pungent as it is in India. Suddenly an awareness shot up my spine ALL IS PERFECT EXACTLY AS IT

IS. It filled my body with a streaming vibration for I-don't-know-how-long—an actual tangible experience, not something I read in a book or idle thoughts of the mind. My life changed forever.

If it's true that everything's perfect in the present moment, LOVE must be here too. If I'm not aware of it my mind and my prejudices are keeping me from knowing. If the present moment is perfect, any person I am with is the Perfect Beloved in this moment. Not necessarily in the next moment, or a month or year from now, but who knows?

Practice seeing whomever you are with in this moment as your Perfect Beloved. If you are sitting at the Coffee Bean and a 50-year old man is sitting next to you, practice saying silently to yourself, "This is my perfect beloved in this moment." If you are receiving a massage and enjoying the stranger's hands caressing your body, say to yourself, "This is my lover in this moment." If you are on a date and are not feeling attracted, (you don't have to be to do this exercise) say to yourself, "In this moment, this is where love is. It is up to me in this moment whether I recognize love or not."

Everything is perfect in the present moment.

This person is my Perfect Beloved in this moment.

This is my lover in this moment.

In this moment, this is where love is.

It is up to me in this moment whether I recognize love or not.

Tantric Mating

Using Tantric Secrets to Create a Relationship Full of Sex, Love and Romance

Tantric Mating
INTRODUCTION

When I met my Perfect Beloved, it looked and felt like magic. We had each been attending a tantra workshop that taught massage techniques and after a few sessions, he asked me to partner with him. What followed, we like to say, was "love at first touch." After a couple of months dating, we decided to be exclusive, then after two years, we got married. We are both always saying, "I didn't know it could be this good."

It seemed like magic when we met because that is what we've been led to believe by movies, fairy tales, Disney princesses and superheroes. It looked and felt like magic because when we met, we both experienced something beyond what we'd ever felt before. Our coming together even seemed like something of the divine. And yet, it wasn't magic because we created it, by preparing ourselves by the inner and outer work we'd each been doing in a dedicated manner for a very long time.

We'd both been on personal and spiritual growth paths for decades. Both of us had received years of therapy and coaching to heal our childhood traumas. Greg had been helped by psychedelics used in a healing capacity. I'd been studying tantra both individually and in groups most of my adult life. For both of us, our personal and spiritual growth was the most important thing in our lives, and in this way, our frequencies matched perfectly.

Osho, the great tantra master, once said, "Tantra is the science of transforming ordinary lovers into soulmates. And that is the grandeur of Tantra. It can transform the whole earth; it can transform each couple into soulmates." I love this quote because it lets us know there is something we can do, that love is not some accident or luck, but that by learning and practicing tantric principles, any serious student of love can create a soulmate relationship like the one Greg and I have.

When you are both on dedicated personal and spiritual growth paths, when you are safe to talk about everything, when the sex is jaw-droppingly exquisite every single time, when you just plain love hanging out together as friends—isn't that what we're all looking for? In this book and the others in the series, I show you how to attract and relish this caliber of a relationship.

There are two parts to *Tantric Mating*: the part you do on yourself before you meet your partner and continue after you find them, and the work you do as a couple. Much of what you can do alone is taught in my book *Tantric Dating: Bringing Love and Awareness to the Dating Process*, which is about turning yourself into a more loving person. I had to do a lot of work on myself to attract love, because as the half-loving person I found myself to be, I could only attract half-loving partners. I wanted more than that and was willing to work for it.

Tantric Mating: Using Tantric Secrets to Create a Relationship Full of Sex, Love and Romance continues the teaching about how to become half of a perfect partnership whether you're single or partnered. Personal and spiritual growth are ongoing, and people who are fully alive are engaged in the process until their last breath. I don't believe we ever come to the endpoint of becoming as fully loving as we can be—but if that completion is possible, it's a goal worth pursuing.

Then there's the part you do together. When Greg and I fell in love, we had to decide what kind of relationship we wanted to create as a couple. Both of us had been in relationships in the past that were painful, and we didn't want to repeat those mistakes. We also had to confront misinformation from the mainstream culture. We found that our intimacy and sex life were enhanced by our best friend status, not diminished.

We found that sex, when there are no resentments lingering between us as a couple, is way beyond conventional expectations. Since the space between us was completely clear, because we had worked on ourselves and carried no resentments, because we had exercised our bodies and kept them healthy and relaxed, even though we were at an age when sex is supposed to have gone downhill, we found ourselves more sexual and more sexually satisfied than ever before. It was shocking and amazing that sex could be this good, even "psychedelic." Nothing we'd heard of before led us to expect this.

In *Tantric Dating*, the secrets of why you haven't found love and how to find it are explained. The third book in the series, *Tantric Relating*, is about how you can communicate both verbally and non- to keep the love fires burning. In this book, *Tantric Mating*, you'll learn how to be in partnership and create your perfect soulmate relationship. You'll find out how soulmates are created and that they do not come to us by magic, how conventional advice has steered us wrong, what kind of work to do on yourself, that tantric sex really is as good as they say, and how to live in a perpetual honeymoon.

And so, I want to teach you my method of *Tantric Mating* that created the soulmate relationship I had dreamed of since childhood, after I found my Perfect Beloved using my *Tantric Dating* method. This book can change your life, your love, and your partner, if they are willing. You must be available to hear truth that is outside the conventional world of advice, for that is not where truth resides. It's up to you to create the soulmate relationship of your dreams. It is within your reach, if only you will reach far enough. When you become the loving person you truly are, love is ever-present.

TANTRIC DATING MINDSET

Soulmates Are Created, Romance Is Created

Millions sit waiting passively for a love that never arrives. Both men and women lie like Sleeping Beauty, hoping they will be kissed and woken up. We dream of a love that enlivens, raises us to an exalted level of being, just like that portrayed in movies, books, songs, and fairy tales. The magical lover will arrive, the Perfect Beloved, the one with whom we will become complete. Finally.

We've been taught to passively wait, and to focus on exteriors. Previously women, but now men in equal numbers as social media has changed the game, spend anxious hours fretting about their appearance and doing whatever they can to improve it. Previously men, but now women in equal numbers, focus on the money it will take to make themselves love-worthy: clothes, cars, cosmetics, cosmetic procedures. We go to the gym, improve our nutrition, learn sex skills online, adopt attitudes from rap, and engage in hookups while we wait.

The beginning of most relationships dangles the promise that the dream romance has finally appeared. Its wonder descends and for a while, from three months to two years, we're entranced. If we're lucky enough that to be in a relationship that lasts that long, often we don't know how to keep it, so we move on, hoping to magically find the dream with someone else. As you know, our relationship breakup rate is now well over 50 percent. That is a lot of heartbreak.

Many of us feel hopeless. I know I certainly felt hopeless before I figured it out. Usually the questions asked are, "Where can I meet men/women? Where is she/he?" We are hoping to be at the right place at the right moment where we will meet (without any effort on our part) and mutually fall in love at first sight, what Hollywood terms the "cute meet." You've seen this moment in numerous rom-coms: the future lovers don't even like each other at first, in fact, they are irritated by each other, but since it was fated and otherworldly all along, they fall in love and live happily ever more.

The problem with these scenarios and the sitting around waiting is that love is not passive at all. You'll never find the love your heart is longing for unless you're willing to work for it. Love and romance are something we create, and no artist of any art form expects to achieve a masterpiece without putting in the effort, discipline, work, mistakes, and steady improvement it takes to get good at anything. No one arrived one night starring at the Hollywood Bowl by sitting and wishing for it to happen. No one has become successful in their career by waiting for a "cute meet."

The fact of the matter is that if you want the sex, love and romance you've always dreamed of, you're going to have to be the one to create it. It's not coming from the sky. You'll have to make it happen. The right question is, "What do I need to do and be to attract and create my perfect love?"

Conventional Expectations

When Greg and I decided to get married, we chose a cute little chapel downtown. We were planning a big party later in the year for friends and family, but for now, we didn't want to wait to make our commitment. We got all dressed up, arrived at our appointed time, and the first order of business was to fill out the paperwork. The woman in charge, who also turned out to be the person who would marry us, within a few minutes asked Greg a question to which he answered, "Yes." Much to our surprise, she responded, "Now that you're getting married, that's how it's going to be from now on: 'Yes, ma'am. No, ma'am.'" We thought maybe she was trying to be amusing but from the look on her face, it didn't appear so.

It continued the whole time we were there. At one point, the woman pointed out that once we were married, "She's the boss." During our ceremony, she noticed I didn't have any flowers and she chided Greg for not getting me any, giving him a mini-lecture on "You have to get her roses, and not just on Valentine's Day."

None of these conventional ideas apply to us whatsoever. Greg knows that if I want flowers, I will buy them. He expresses his romantic feelings frequently in a way that fits for him and for me, and neither of us is "the boss." It was really weird to have these conventional expectations about love and marriage show up in so tender a moment that was supposed to be about us.

Around the same time, we had a guy remodeling our home, and Greg was supervising. I don't usually care too much about the details in the house, except for certain things. Greg pointed out to the guy that he had fitted a tile wrong, and he responded, "Oh, she's not going to like that." Greg explained that I really don't care about stuff like that. The next day when the handyman showed up for work, the first thing he said to Greg was, "Was she mad about the tile? Did you get in trouble? You know how women are."

Where is this all coming from? Conventional expectations. For many people, this is the story they have in their heads when they interact.

If you turn on the television for a few hours, there are constant messages and images about all kinds of ideas that may or may not be true. There are jokes and storylines about the supposed "war" between men and women. We are constantly told that men are inconsiderate slobs who only want sex, not intimacy or affection. Women rarely want sex; just leave them alone. Your life is basically over once you're in a committed relationship, and if you get married, you're never having sex again. Once married, you don't want to see each other and all you're going to do is fight. All of these messages and images create a mindset and behavior that have been normalized by mainstream culture so much so that we often think they're true without even questioning them.

One of the first things we want to do is to identify what conventional expectations about sex, love and romance we have adopted from the mainstream culture that may not be true and challenge them.

The Work You Do on Your Own

Whether you are single or partnered, you'll need to work on yourself to create Tantric Mating, but not in the way you think. We've been told many untruths, such as it's all about improving our appearance, or being more youthful or slim, or owning more stuff, but that's not how you find or create love. Love is a question of frequency, and the higher yours is, the higher the frequency of the relationship you'll be able to attract and create.

Ways to raise our frequency can be thought of holistically in different arenas: the physical, emotional, financial, and spiritual. Physically, you'll want a fit and lively body to make love, go on walks together, give and receive massages, and enjoy the activities of daily life until well past the age when most people expect to be old. That means you'll need to clean up your food and exercise. If you want more than average results, you'll have to pay more than average attention.

Then we must consider how you feel about your body. You won't be able to have great sex if you haven't learned to love your own shape and discarded any nonsense from the culture that bodies aren't beautiful the way they are. Stop following social media that promotes body shaming, ageism, and materialism; instead, choose to follow those that promote loving values.

Raising the frequency of our emotional life involves dealing with any baggage from the past, so clean that stuff up. If you had a difficult childhood and thus difficult relationships afterward, you'll most likely benefit from therapy.

Here are some questions to ask yourself to assess your emotional maturity: Are you an independent, non-codependent adult? Are you able to soothe your own feelings of loneliness, fear, doubt, insecurity? Are you emotionally reactive, meaning, when you get mad, do you yell, break things, throw tantrums? Are you disrespectful toward others? If you don't want these things in your love life, best to make sure they are weeded out of yourself.

Are you financially stable? It's not necessary to be wealthy or have a lot of money, but it is important to be able to pay your bills and have little to no debt. If you are not covering the basics and haven't put anything away for a rainy day, it will show up in feelings of insecurity and low self-esteem. To attract stable love, make sure your own life is stable.

If you want someone who is ready to make a full commitment, ask yourself if you have made a full commitment to your career, a pet, your own life? If you're unsure, in flux, or waiting to find a partner before making important decisions, you'll attract a person who's unsure about you whether you are single or partnered.

The best thing you can do to attract and maintain love is to make sure that you are a loving person. If you are only a halfway-loving person, you will attract a person who is only half-loving. Ask yourself, "Am I soulmate material?" and if there are areas listed above that need attention, do your work until the answer is yes. You don't need to be perfect, but if you dream of perfect love, or as we are calling it Tantric Mating, you are half of that equation.

Friendship Is Required for Tantric Sex

Word on the street is that "the friend zone" is the dead end of romantic possibility and certainly not where you'll find great sex. That may be true if what you're seeking is a wild weekend with a fantasy figure, which often includes, if you've bought into conventional daydreams, the delicious pain of being rejected afterward. If this type of rainbow beginning ever does "work out," you will always be wondering if your partner really loves you or if it's a relationship based on appearances because deep trust has not been established.

Dr. John Gottman, a psychologist in Seattle and big kahuna relationship guru, has been conducting research in his "Love Lab" for decades on what makes relationships work. He observed and measured couples with the aid of electrodes as they got along, argued, had fun. His wife, Dr. Judy Gottman, a practicing psychotherapist, put his research results into action with her clients, and together they have developed trainings for therapists and written best-selling books.

One of the most jaw-dropping findings of the Gottmans is that 69 percent of people in successful partnerships rate the friendship as the most important element. When I first heard this, I was stunned. I had been brainwashed to believe that men would rate sex as by far the most important thing, but the majority do not.

If friendship is the most important component of a successful relationship, why have we not been emphasizing it? Encouraging it? Helping people enhance it? Why are singles being told to avoid being "in the friend zone" at all costs? Someone who is our best friend is exactly who we should be looking for and what we should be growing in our partnerships.

If you want to be really relaxed in bed, if you want to feel free to be creative, if you want to know you will not be shamed, that your good qualities will be appreciated and your not-so overlooked, if you want to snuggle and hug and not be judged on your performance, and to know with absolute certainty that your lover will not leave you if you gain five pounds, you'll need to cultivate the quality of best-friendship with your lover.

To relax enough into the mystery for tantric sex to occur, you'll need to build total trust. You both need to know that anything that happens will be okay, that you are not being judged but rather honored and held, and that anything that comes up is welcome.

This applies if you are single as well. You can be friends and friendly with a one-night stand, a short-term relationship or a long one. That quality of friendliness comes from you. You care about sharing, honoring, and having fun. Not some heavy breathing, pain-filled horror show of people using one other to enhance their egos.

Osho said, "Friendship is higher than love." In the year that I lived at the tantra ashram, friendship always came first. Friendship doesn't diminish sexuality; it enhances sexuality. Many people say they don't agree, but when I ask them, "Have you ever had really intimate sex?" they invariably answer that, no, they have not. For soul-stirring, heart-centered, really intimate tantric sex, friendship is a prerequisite.

Safety Is the Root of Everything

All extraordinary relationships and phenomenal sex are based on a foundation of safety. In tantra, we say that this stems from the root or the base chakra, down close to your tailbone. This safety is the root of the tree of your relationship with others and the world. There are three areas to consider: your own safety, your partner's, and the safety of the relationship.

First, when considering your own safety, do you feel safe in the world? If your childhood was not a safe place, you may grow up feeling insecure. If you experienced sexual molestation or assault, more likely than not, you won't find sex to be safe. You may have been taught not to trust men or women or gender-fluid people. To heal these issues, revisiting them in psychotherapy may help.

You may not feel safe if you are not in the best physical health, or because you fear aging and losing your attractiveness. (We don't lose our attractiveness with age unless we believe we do, but that's for another book.)

Another facet of considering our own safety is, are you safe for other people? Is another person safe with you? Can they be sure you will not diss them behind their back? Are you the kind of person who is there when needed, or are you a fair-weather friend? Can your partner trust you to speak your truth? Are you hiding something that if your partner found out, they would be hurt?

Secondly, consider if your partner, or the person you are considering for a partner, is a safe person. This may take some time to deduce. Certainly, you want to make sure they are not physically or sexually abusive, but also not emotionally unkind, meaning you can trust they will not make fun of you, deride or shame you, or be overly sensitive or reactive.

Building a safe relationship means that when together, you are able to be your true selves. It means that when you are ready for intimacy, you have created a safe space free from interruption. It means making agreements so that you know what to expect, and that the two of you are on the same page.

New lovers need to take time to learn to feel safe with each other. However, even couples who have been together for twenty-five years may find that they don't trust each other right now. Trust and safety are works in progress, and their maintenance is ongoing.

In a previous relationship, I didn't feel safe with my partner because I suspected he was flirting with other women over text and social media. Because of that, I decided early on in my relationship with Greg that I didn't want that for us. I let him know that there was nothing I had to hide, there would be no one I would be flirting with, and that he had full access to my phone or email if he wanted to check. I also decided to always report to him whenever some guy doesn't realize I'm married and flirts with me. I don't have to do this, but I want Greg to feel absolutely safe and secure. Greg has never asked to see my phone or email—he doesn't have to, and I don't have to look at his either. This is just one of our practices that has established complete safety with each other.

Safety is needed to be able to fully relax in one another's presence. Relaxation is the key to intimacy and great sex.

Soulmate Creation and the Centers

Osho said that soulmate creation has to do with the centers being aligned. First, we'll take a look at what the centers are, and then in the next chapter, how to get them into alignment. Tantra uses the word "chakras," but many people are uncomfortable with Sanskrit terms, so we'll use the word "centers" instead.

There are seven centers in the body, placed along the spine, starting at the tailbone. These centers are not actual physical entities, although they do seem to line up with the glands of the endocrine system. People of higher vision and wisdom have seen them as spinning centers of energy. When they are whirling freely, each energy center can be experienced as free and unblocked. Everyone differs in the level of development in each of their centers, and in their level of development compared with others.

1. We previously talked about how the root or base center is concerned with safety, the safety required for all trusting relationships and for tantric sex. The first center is about security, vitality, and whether we feel good about being alive. A person who has moved around a lot might not feel safe and secure, or someone who's experienced trauma may have challenges establishing a sense of rootedness, connectedness, and commitment to life.

2. The second center is located around the genitals and is about sexuality and emotions. (Anybody notice that emotions and sex are often connected?) It is just about impossible to grow up in this culture and not have unresolved issues about sex. Most couples are unmatched in terms of how often they want sex, what kind, and differences in each person's past experience.

3. The third center resides in the belly and is about power, personal and otherwise. One reason we've had trouble in our relationships is because of the power struggles going on. I was taught in graduate school that the power struggle stage lasts for the first twenty-three years of the relationship. I don't know if that's true or not, as I've never been in a relationship of that length, but I do know that it's possible to avoid power struggles if each person has developed their own sense of personal power. If you look out in the world, a lot of power struggles are going on all over the planet.

4. Some people think that the world as a whole is trying to wake up in the fourth center, the heart center. You can really notice the difference between people whose heart centers are beginning to open, those who are living from the heart, wanting to spread love, and those who haven't gotten there yet. We've all got a long way to go to blossom fully into love.

5. The fifth center is in the throat and is about truth speaking. Most of us have large blocks in this center from trying not to speak our truth from fear of being misunderstood or because it's not going to be politically correct. We may not speak because we know the corporate world doesn't want to hear what we have to say. Many of us have been outsiders, so we have kept quiet about our beliefs and opinions. Many relationship "experts" (not me) teach that there are things you're supposed to say and things you shouldn't so people will be attracted to you. We've all grown up with that idea since high school.

6. The sixth center is in the middle of the forehead and is about true seeing, vision and philosophy. As it's rare for relationships to be hampered by this and the next center, we won't be spending much time on them.

7. The seventh center at the top of our head relates to our sense of spirituality and connection to the divine.

Take the time right now to assess where you are. The more we work on ourselves and the areas of our lives that these centers represent, the freer and more energetic we become.

The higher you are in your development, the higher the frequency of the partner you will attract and the greater your chances of creating the soulmate relationship of your dreams. Where are you in the development of your centers?

Soulmates' Centers Are Aligned

In soulmate relationships, the centers are aligned, meaning, the development of each center in one person is mirrored back by the partner's. Ideally, we would have an individual with perfect flowering in every center meeting another perfect person, but of course that never happens. Each of us is more advanced in one center than another, and we all have room to grow. What you can do is to work individually on evolving your own centers, and when in a relationship, work together to strengthen and bring yourselves into alignment. The more areas you match up, the more likely the relationship has soulmate potential.

The problems in relationships can be described as misalignments in these centers. An example is that two people meet and one person has a more developed heart center and wants a heart connection, while the other person's sex center is developed but not their heart. Another example is that many couples get stuck with underdeveloped power centers and so are madly trying to be one-up all the time, and find they are not able to speak truth to one another.

Center imbalances can show up in other ways. For example, a lot of so-called spiritual people are in what we call spiritual bypass. Their upper centers are open: They are very spiritual, praying and meditating, fasting, worrying about maintaining a pure vegan diet and so forth, but they don't have a job or are unkind to others. They need to work on maturing their lower centers so that they have a good solid foundation to support a relationship.

The first thing to do is to assess where you are with your center development. The second is to work on boosting them, because the more advanced the centers, the happier you will be, and the closer you will be to soulmate creation. Here are some suggestions:

1. First Center (Safety): Wake up your body and your aliveness, practice Osho Kundalini Meditation, beautify your home, ask yourself frequently, "Am I in my body? Am I safe?" take steps to establish ongoing safety for yourself and others, shake your booty and stamp your feet.

2. Second Center (Sex and Emotions): Learn sexual skills, basic through advanced, deprogram yourself from conventional sexual conditioning, clear past trauma with a therapist, overcome cultural shaming, live life sex-positively.

3. Third Center (Power): Take 100 percent responsibility for your results and your life, get yourself to a place where you can say, "My life works," become financially stable.

4. Fourth Center (Heart): Adopt a pet, learn to be universally social, donate time and/or money to a charity that inspires you,

practice kindheartedness, repair things with your family.

5. Fifth Center (Truth Speaking): Learn to speak with authenticity; join groups where genuine speaking is encouraged and supported, for example, Twelve-Step groups or group therapy; make agreements with your partner about how much truth you want to share in your relationships.

Begin with maximizing the first five centers. Without the development of these areas, the relationship will not have strong enough legs to support it. After that, you can focus on expanding the higher centers: intuition, true seeing, and spirituality.

Working on your centers takes place both individually and as a couple. If you are single, the more your centers are strengthened, the higher the frequency of a partner you will attract. And when you are in a relationship, use this guide to raise your partnership to the elevation of soulmates.

Orgasm Is Not What You Think

Orgasm is not what you think. We've been brainwashed by the conventional culture to believe that orgasm is something it's not. This indoctrination is so pervasive we don't even question the notion that orgasm is the goal of sex. It's part of what it is, but that's not the whole understanding.

We've been taught that the point of sexual play with another being is to stimulate each other with increasing intensity to the point of orgasm. Conventional sex goes like this: foreplay, she comes, he comes, it's over. For non-hetero couples, negotiation is required, but the blueprint remains the same. This is, of course, better than historical sex where the female's pleasure was disregarded, but this pattern we're supposed to perform gets very boring. We've even been provided with bar graphs to show us how our arousal should go up, up, up, and then drop off, as if this is optimal.

In this type of sex, every movement is geared toward the eventual orgasm. Everything is leading up to it with tension and strain. The more intense it is, the better. Women are expected to come every time like men do, and if they don't, everyone is grumpy. The idea is that orgasm is something to strive for, that it takes effort, and we often find ourselves disappointed, again. It becomes a performance marker for how good the sex is.

This style of sex has been the mainstream model since the 1970s when it was deified by Masters and Johnson. Yes, there have always been people who enjoyed this type of sex, but it was not always considered the end-all and be-all. Masters and Johnson began studying arousal in laboratories, measuring it, and so forth. Thus began the conventional codification of lovemaking—that it should look like this, act like that, and take this particular path to completion. I don't think laboratory sex knows anything about the essence of sex, and this research has created a complete misunderstanding of sexuality.

Something more profound has been going on since the beginning of time—what we call *tantra*. Let me share with you how I discovered this. Soon after I arrived in India at the tantra ashram where I was to live for a year, I was lying relaxing on my bed. My breath began to deepen and circle in a loop from my nostrils to my tailbone with no beginning or end. Without any intention, a part of me surrendered, and the breathing started happening by itself. Orgasmic waves rushed through my body … pulsating—it was so enjoyable.

Days later, I went to an event called Energy Darshan. Music was playing, and everyone was dancing vigorously. All of a sudden, completely unexpectedly, an energy shot up my spine and my vagina began contracting. I realized, oh my God, I'm having an orgasm! How could this be? I was having an energy orgasm just from dancing, not from a partner or from touching myself.

Over the course of that year, there were several times when unexpected orgasms would bless me. In *Tantric Dating*, I recounted an incident at the Burning Ghats when out of the blue, an orgasm rushed up my spine, and I felt overwhelming joy. I had hitched a ride on the orgasm wave.

Orgasm is actually a pulsating frequency that is always going on in the universe, buzzing and humming underneath everything. It is a level of bliss that never stops. When we engage in conventional sex where we struggle, get to the orgasm, and poof! it's gone—we have come up and met this frequency briefly.

When you choose not to have conventional sex and instead practice tantra, you can learn to catch a ride on the orgasm wave, and then it doesn't stop. It can last for minutes or hours or days. It depends on your level of development, your relaxation, and your capacity for bliss. It's possible to lift your own frequency by the practice of tantric exercises, certain ways of making love, particular ways of breathing, and then you can surf along this vibrating frequency. You catch it. You ride it. You know if you let go, you can always catch a wave again.

This is what orgasm is. This knowledge has been withheld from you by people who don't have a clue. I want you to experience this level of orgasm because once you do, you will want it in your life. There's no doubt about that.

Sacred Sexuality

In tantra, sex is sacred, as is the body. This is a radically different attitude than the one most of us grew up with. The majority of us learned that sex is naughty and that pleasure is something we need to sneak. The conventional worldview of the last two thousand years has been that the body is sinful; thus sex and pleasure are too. We've learned to live ignoring our bodies, which encourages people to walk around as merely heads—looking, thinking, analyzing, and judging—rather than feeling the wisdom that the body can bring.

One of the first tasks of Tantric Mating is to befriend your body and those of your lover(s) and honor them as sacred. When you do so, it's possible to gaze in amazement at their breathtaking beauty, their seemingly endless capacity for pleasure, and their innate wisdom. When you hold sex as sacred, you begin to honor your partner, your body and theirs, your sexual organs, your pleasure, and the space you make love in as manifestations of the divine.

As a tantric practice, you can remember to remember that you are embodied, that this moment is sacred, that this man or woman is my beloved in this moment, and that these sexual feelings are sacred. You can cultivate these attitudes within yourself and through practice become more open to love and to life. It's a discipline like any other, such as learning to play tennis or chess or how to speak French.

Osho once said that the best sex is had by meditators. Meditation is a practice of touching the sacred in daily life. I believe what Osho meant was that tantric people are practicing mindfulness while we have sex. Consciously, we're staying in the present moment, not trying to get somewhere in the future. We're not thinking about lunch, or the news, or the multiplication tables, which is what they teach men to do so they won't come so quickly. (Thanks, guys, for doing that, but we'd rather have your presence.) We're not trying to get to orgasm; we're too busy enjoying the present moment. Just to touch each other's hands mindfully is making love.

When you are fully embodied as you touch another's flesh, you can notice when you aren't present or when you are spacing out. As a practice, you can remind yourself to stay present as much as possible and bring that to lovemaking. Always you come back to the present moment with full awareness, just as we do in meditation.

By practicing mindful, sacred sex with your lover, you may share an experience of the divine. You may even participate in what might be called "psychedelic sex." It all depends on letting go of what the conventional culture has taught you about unloving, mechanical sex, and bringing heart, love, and mindfulness to lovemaking, plus a sense of worshipping your beloved as a god or goddess.

Sex Is a Conversation

Sex is a conversation, a wordless exchange. Everything between you and your partner and all things enveloping the two of you are there in the bedroom. Every aspect gets communicated: the level of your commitment, whether or not you are able to open in vulnerability and trust, your ability to hold or not hold each other's gaze, or if you can let go and let the bodies make love instead of the minds. Sex is a conversation between lovers about what they mean to each other. Every touch, stroke, heartbeat, endearment, and sigh conveys a message.

During sex, you are also communicating nonverbally about the difficulties in your relationship. Boredom, untruths, withholds, and conversations that have not been had will show up as "I'm not in the mood" or less-than-stellar lovemaking. Sometimes when making love brings you back into that state of being so close, looking into each other's eyes, intimate and safe, it transcends those problems. Sometimes it doesn't.

Men, it seems, often prefer to speak through the language of sex rather than through talking. Men express love through their penis, which is a beautiful thing about men. We've been brainwashed that this is something terrible—that men only want "one thing." It's quite beautiful, really, but in a sex-negative culture, we're not able to see that. Men want to express love sexually. They're looking to share it in the way that men convey love.

It's a tantric perspective that sex and love can be the same thing. But because of our cultural programming, we're not able to see that this is the way men are driven to love and connection. Neither men nor women have been taught this. Men want to share themselves. They want to express.

What if we interpreted men's desire for sexual connection as the hunger to connect, instead of, oh, he just wants sex? What if connection through sex is beautiful rather than a negative thing? A man wanting to have sex is often a bid for intimacy and love.

This is not meant to imply that if you just have sex, it will take care of all your problems. Sometimes when the conversation seems to be going nowhere, you can open yourself to the possibility that a beautiful conversation about your relationship can be had while you're making love.

Sex is a language we have that isn't verbal. It's a communication, a way to express love and to work out problems. It's a way to reconnect without having to do all this psychologizing. Much of the time, it's much more effective.

Psychedelic Sex

Tantric sex is as good as you've heard it is. It has little resemblance, however, to the conventional style of sex which consists of effort, tension, focus on the goal of orgasm, explosion and release, and when it's over, both parties are spent.

If sex is not about the goal of orgasm, what do you have? You have the sensual pleasure of being in this exquisite space with your lover, awareness of their touch, breath, and movement, the spiritual connection between you, and the promise of growing intimacy. You have the realization that this present moment is all there is. The partner is your beloved, your perfect love, your soulmate. Your being together is actually generating more love in the world, rather than the energy being discharged in the sex act. You have the opportunity to learn to sustain a state of pleasure and bliss for longer periods of time, instead of ending quickly because your nervous system hasn't yet learned to tolerate that much happiness.

Tantrikas (people who practice tantra) have told of altered states while having sex for hours that are similar to those brought about by psychedelic drugs. There are reports of sex being mind-shattering, life-changing, and reality-altering. People say they have felt an all-encompassing sense that this sexual union comes from a divine source, a perception of merging with their partner. Some people disclose that they've seen gods and goddesses in the bedroom, or energy and light. Some have talked about time traveling or remembering past lives, a sense of divine union, or experiencing ecstasies more powerful than orgasm. Tantric sex and psychedelics have in common being anchored in the present moment, experiencing altered states, and the possibilities for bliss, transcendence, and healing.

When you make love without the goal of orgasm, every touch to the skin is different—it has no intention other than to enjoy the moment. You can relax into protracted pleasuring of each other. When you have conventional sex, you will usually be finished in about twenty minutes or less. In tantric sex, if we want to cultivate "psychedelic" experiences without the use of psychedelic drugs, we have noticed the following timings:

- After 45 minutes, the mind falls silent
- After 2 hours, certain phenomena appear
- After 3 hours, a heightening of psychedelic phenomena
- After a certain amount of time, the bodies start making love by themselves
- 6–10 hours of lovemaking are possible, a whole weekend

Greg and I rarely decide to have an orgasm. Instead, we prefer to hitch a ride on the orgasmic waves that carry us blissfully along for who-knows-how-long.

Creating Magic

You know it's you, right?, who's responsible for creating the magic in your relationship—not your partner, Tinkerbell, or the goddess of love. The good news is that there are so many ways to up the magic quotient and increase the likelihood of living happily ever after. Here are some tantric suggestions:

- First of all, choose a partner you can trust. Whether you've been together for years or have recently met, you'll need to share deep trust with your partner in order to create magic. If there are conversations you need to have to reestablish trust, schedule them now. If this seems daunting, hire a competent marriage and family therapist to help.

- Clear your relationship. Anything still nagging you from the past with your partner, whether it was this morning or months ago, will keep the magic from happening. It will also show up in the bedroom. These are conversations that need to be had, and keep being had, so that your relationship stays clear from unspoken resentment and unhappiness. (This is covered in detail in my book, *Tantric Relating*.)

- Cultivate an attitude of gratitude and devotion to your partner. Become thankful that this partner chooses to be with you, and express it frequently. Choose to focus on your partner's divinity rather than, like most people, their flaws.

- Make plenty of time. A relationship takes time: time to hang out, time to plan, time to make love. Many people today need to prioritize their relationship and schedule time together and make dates.

- Make a sacred space. The bedroom is a good place to start as this is where you make love. Do you have beautiful linens that feel good to your skin? Plump, comfy pillows? Art on the walls that reflects an environment of beauty and sexuality? Create a magic bedroom devoid of anything other than that which promotes sleep or lovemaking.

- When you touch, focus awareness inside your own body, or where your partner is touching. Notice, as you would while meditating, when your attention is in the past or the future, and gently bring it back to the present moment with your partner. That mindfulness brings gentle magic to being together and to touch.

- Create playlists of music that is intoxicating to make love to. It is usually recommended to use music without words, or words in a foreign language so you're not distracted. For tantric sex, music that is calming and meditative is preferred so as to stay slow and relaxed. Most conventional "sexy music" encourages tension and release. Experiment and find out what is best for you.

- Be in your body, not your head. Magic occurs when we drop down into our bodies and leave thinking behind. Mental chatter can easily destroy connecting.

- Drop the idea of "foreplay." In tantra, we give up the idea that how we pleasure ourselves before intercourse is somehow less important. We find all actions of lovemaking equally pleasurable and sacred, and we may not even do these things "before." Tantrikas don't feel the need to follow the conventional formula for sex.

- Enjoy protracted pleasuring. Increase your ability to enjoy giving and receiving touch for its own sake, and not as an avenue for getting somewhere else (orgasm). This ability is a muscle that can be gotten into shape, and the practice is more fun than the gym.

- Go with whatever arises. Learn to relax and be with what is, rather than what conventional sex says you ought to be doing.

- Praise. Tell your partner when they look hot, or do a kind thing, or turn you on. Tell them frequently. Look for excuses to praise them. I've never heard of anyone saying, "Please! Stop telling me good things about myself!"

- "My only intention is to be fully present." Rather than being goal-oriented to sometime in the future, or trying to make something happen, tantra suggests we only intend to be fully present in the now.

- Practice eye gazing. When you look deeply into another person's eyes, it is impossible not to fall in love with them. Perhaps this is why we are afraid to do it. When I was in India at the tantra ashram, we did exercises where we looked into each other's eyes for twenty minutes, and we all couldn't stop crying—we fell in love with everyone in the room no matter what they looked like or who they were. This is perhaps a clue for how to create more magic and love in our partnerships and in the world.

Building and Maintaining Your Soulmate Status

"And they lived happily ever after." That little phrase from our favorite fairy tales sets us up for disappointment when our relationships don't glide on magically without effort on our parts. It's not exactly like that, is it? Instead, when we hear it's going to take work to maintain our relationships, that sounds like it's going to be difficult and treacherous. It may be if that's how you set it up, or it can be fun, sexy, and delightful.

First off, it requires maintaining the high frequency state you were in to be able to attract this great partner. That means continuing to attend to your physical health, your vitality, and your emotional stability, so that you're not flying off the handle about every little thing. It means staying interested in your life, being invested in something greater than yourself, such as your career or volunteer work. You must have passion for life to have a passionate relationship.

Secondly, it takes using and expanding your communication skills. This is so essential that the third book in the series, *Tantric Relating*, will go into it deeply, but for now, let's just say that every little challenge that gets swept under the carpet and not discussed will show up in the bedroom as "I'm not in the mood" or resentment against your partner. This leads to the conventional wisdom that it's inevitable that sex will decrease after the first two years of being together. But it is possible for you to nurture a really exciting sex life, and that's going to take attention as it doesn't happen just by itself.

Thirdly, you need to make time. Our lives are so busy, and if we don't prioritize intimate relations, they won't happen. If you'd rather just watch Netflix in the evening because it's easier, that's what your relationship will turn into. It's not a bad choice if that's what you want. But if your heart's desire is for a soulmate relationship with intimate, evolving sexuality, then that's going to require dedicated time.

Fourth, it's important to set goals for your relationship. What do you want to do together? What are your priorities? Travel, or would you rather design an oasis in the backyard? What are you up to as a couple?

Every year I make my personal goals, and then get together with Greg to make goals for our relationship. Last year we took up qigong and trained for a half-marathon. What do you want to do this year? Is there something you want to study together?

So again, there are the two aspects of maintaining your soulmate status: your own personal growth as well as your growth as a couple. What are you doing to maintain your half of the couple? And what are you doing together to cultivate and grow that? It is a project, if you want to look at it that way, a project of creating the soulmate relationship you've always dreamed of. Everyone's dreaming of it, but guess what? You make it happen.

A Perpetual Honeymoon

Consider for a moment the word "honeymoon." You will discover a subtle brainwashing that says the beginning of a relationship is romantic and blissful, and the rest of it is not. The message is that you're going to be high on sexual attraction and love for a short period of time, and after that, it tanks. The very word "honeymoon" sets up an expectation that relationships inevitably go downhill.

This expectation of decline may dovetail with seeing your parents not having the soulmate relationship you dream of. Many of us grew up with people who fought a lot, some to the point of splintering the family by getting divorced. Other parents were asleep to each other, seemingly half-dead or on automatic pilot, which happens when there's a lot that's unspoken. Many people have never witnessed juicy, alive, long-term relationships, so they don't know it's possible. I've even had people ask me, "Do happy couples exist?"

Emphatically, yes. The higher possibilities were first shown to me years ago when I attended a party in Beverly Glen, an affluent neighborhood in the hills above Los Angeles. I was excited as I walked in because the gathering was for single people pursuing personal and spiritual growth. As always back then, I was searching for my true love and thought I might find him there. Instead of meeting him that night, what I experienced is still inspiring me today. Sitting and glowing with an unearthly radiance was an older couple, surprisingly sexy and hot. I had never seen any two people, let alone any one, so alive and full of energy! It was as if they were in the foreground and everyone else, backstage.

At that time, I still believed in the conventional ageism that older people aren't interested in sex.

These two appeared to be on their honeymoon even though they had been together for years. I had to know what they knew and wanted to have what they had, so I went up and introduced myself. They knew secrets for sure—they were *tantrikas*, people who practice tantra. Seeing and being around their heightened energy was part of what set me out on my own journey of studying tantra and creating my perfect soulmate relationship. I ended up living in their house and learning from them, but that's for another book.

It was enlivening just to be in their presence. That's what a soulmate relationship can do—bring inspiration and more aliveness to those around them. From meeting this high-frequency couple, I knew sex and relationships could get better with age. Now, my husband and I are that couple.

You have the power to create your relationship to be a honeymoon that lasts, or you can slide into the aftermath that follows the conventional honeymoon. It really depends on what you and your partner want to create. If you want to have a wild, sexual, romantic ride, you can create that. If you don't mind that the romance and the sexuality decline with age and longevity, you can create that too. It's completely up to you. There's not some nebulous thing called a relationship that's out of your control, that's going to do what it wants. It's up to you and your partner.

By the way, how did you create your honeymoon if you had one? Or if you haven't, how do you imagine you would?

- You spent time planning activities that would delight the both of you.
- You allocated money and time to make it fabulous.
- You were on your best behavior—kind, humorous, full of praise.
- You focused on what was best about your partner—their body, their generosity, their integrity—and left the criticism in the trash where it belongs.

- You went out of your way to perform little romantic gestures.
- You made the effort to look your best.
- You dedicated exclusive time and space to you, your lover, and your love life.

If you decide you're going to create a perpetual honeymoon, these actions might be a good place to start.

Dedicated to Personal and Spiritual Growth

You now have all you need to create and maintain a soulmate relationship using the mindset and methods of Tantric Mating. The question is, will you do it? You must live your life dedicated to personal and spiritual growth and support this in your partner. You'll need to understand that growth is sometimes painful and that going through rough spots is often a good sign that you are growing. If you are increasingly expanding in the seven centers, if you are practicing seeing the divine in your partner, if you are excited to explore new ways of sexuality, you will create your Perfect Beloved and your soulmate relationship.

Some of you have been on the personal and spiritual growth path for years, while some of you are entering it now. It's all good. You're going to want to dedicate yourself to this growth for the rest of your life. The opportunity for more never stops. Osho, famed tantra master, says we have until our last breath to continue to evolve.

We talked in *Tantric Dating* about how if you're single, you'll want to be working on yourself, your physical health, your emotional stability, your financial wealth, your judgmental-ness, becoming a heart-centered person, and cultivating a more spiritual attitude toward others. You'll need to reject the methods the mainstream culture teaches to look for a partner, open your heart, and engage in personal work.

In *Tantric Relating*, we'll talk more about how to communicate verbally and nonverbally to create and keep your soulmate relationship alive. As a couple, you might choose activities to share together that promote personal and spiritual growth. The two of you may take hikes together to get lost in the splendor of nature. You may want to study and master some area of knowledge together, maybe take a class or tantra workshop to learn more about how to relate intimately and sexually.

I know that since my partner and I are both committed to our personal and spiritual growth paths that our relationship can only get better over time. There's a raft of societal brainwashing that sex, love, and romance only get worse as you get older. If you're both dedicated to personal and spiritual growth, it can only improve as you solve life's problems and create your life exactly as you want it. That is possible for you and is your future if you choose it.

TANTRIC MATING EXERCISES

EXERCISE #1: Challenging the Conventional Mindset

To become a free human being, it's essential to examine conventional beliefs and expectations and discard those that don't fit the world you want to create. Take some time and think through these commonly held "truths," and consider if you want to keep believing them or throw them out. Write your preferred attitude in the space below. An example of an alternative mindset is offered for the first conventional teaching.

- Young people are more attractive than older people.

    Example: Attractiveness is actually enhanced by age due to a person's increasing sense of wisdom, self-esteem, and life mastery.

- The definition of who is "attractive" should be defined by advertising and social media.
- I can't help who I'm attracted to—it's in my DNA.
- Conventionally good-looking people are better candidates for love.
- Men want sex; women want love.
- Friendship means the death of sexual attraction.
- Marriage means sex goes downhill.
- People get less interested in sex as they get older, and if they don't, it's kind of gross.
- A sign of true love is that your partner can read your mind and fulfill your wishes without you having to do or say anything.
- Soulmates happen magically—it's either a soulmate relationship or it's not, and there's nothing you can do about it.
- Men lose freedom in marriage ("the old ball and chain").

- One person becomes the boss in the relationship. If it's the woman, the man's masculinity is in question.
- There exists a war between the sexes.
- Traditional sex roles should be reverted to for relationships to work.
- Everyone else is having great, trouble-free sex.
- I can't find a soulmate because I am too … (short, fat, old, poor, smart …).
- It means men don't love their partners if they don't do traditional things such as buy roses.
- Relationships are hard.
- Love happens by magic, and the best thing you can do is wait passively for its arrival.
- It's my partner's responsibility to keep the love, sex, and romance going in the relationship.

EXERCISE #2:
Are You Soulmate Material?

The following is a questionnaire I developed for a matchmaking firm. How do you score? Is someone dreaming of you as their Perfect Beloved?

Physical

Are you still wearing clothes from 5 to 10 years ago?

Are you wearing old-people clothes?

Do you have an up-to-date haircut?

Are you sexy?

Do you have some kind of exercise routine?

Emotional

Do you have unresolved issues from your childhood?

Are you clinging to a past love? Are you still in love with someone?

Do you feel like it's okay to take out your frustrations on other people?

Financial

Are you financially stable?

Do you realize that anyone you marry will be responsible for your debt?

Are you in financial integrity?

Mental

Are you keeping up on current events, cultural and political, at least enough to converse?

Have you read a book in the past year? The past month?

Social

Do you have enough friends?

Are you universally social?

Do you have an interesting life that someone would like to join? Or are you a couch potato?

Home

Would your dream lover feel comfortable in your home?

Is your bedroom sexy?

When was the last time you bought new sheets? A new bedspread?

Spiritual

When did you last feel awe at the beauty of the universe?

Have you handled any addictions you might have?

Do you make any financial contributions to causes that inspire you? Do any charity work?

EXERCISE #3:
The #1 Thing You Can Do to Improve Your Relationships

Feeling unappreciated is one of the main reasons people give for why they leave jobs and relationships. That's why it's so refreshing to hear what someone else appreciates about us. How nice is it to think of an oasis where someone is noticing what we do right.

The number one thing you can do today to improve your relationships is to tell someone what you appreciate about them. Not just a compliment like, "You look nice today," although under the right circumstances, that's always good. The trick is to use the word "appreciate" because that's what people are starving for, being appreciated. It is actually better if you notice a small thing because it is unexpected, and the person gets to feel that you are noticing and approving of them.

Simple examples might be, "I appreciate that you took our son to the ball game." "I appreciate that you take time for yourself, which allows me to do the same." "I appreciate that you take out the garbage before you're asked."

Mark and Diane were seeing me for marriage counseling because they were fighting and criticizing each other bitterly. I asked Mark to change gears and tell his wife something he appreciated about her. Diane waited nervously while Mark struggled to identify something, as this was a new way for him to think. When he finally said, "I appreciate that you dress so well for work," she broke out into a huge smile that looked as if he had given her a dozen roses. She hadn't known Mark was even paying attention.

Give it a try. Let your significant other off the hook and tell him or her a small thing you appreciate. Call your mother and give her "an appreciation." Let your employee know that you appreciate that she is always on time. Everyone can use a dose.

Give someone the gift of appreciation today and watch your relationships blossom.

EXERCISE #4: Raise Your Frequency by Working on Your Centers

You've learned that soulmates' centers are aligned, and that the quality of your relationship depends on the work you do on your own. Now is your chance to create your action plan, and raise your frequency to the level of the relationship you are seeking. Go back to the chapter explaining the centers, circle the actions that need attention, add ideas of your own, and create and implement your plan. Be sure to have fun—growth is a lifelong journey to be enjoyed.

My Action Plan:

First Center (Safety, Physical Body)

Second Center (Sex and Emotions)

Third Center (Power)

Fourth Center (Heart)

Fifth Center (Truth Speaking)

EXERCISE #5:
Atisha Heart Meditation

"You will be surprised if you do [this meditation]. The moment you take all the sufferings of the world inside you, they are no longer sufferings. The heart immediately transforms the energy. The heart is a transforming force: drink in misery, and it is transformed into blissfulness."
—Osho, The Book of Wisdom

Bringing your awareness to your body and breathing, feel yourself here and now. Then bring your awareness to your heart chakra, the energy center in the middle of your chest. If it helps you, place one or both of your hands on your heart center. Absorb each in-breath into the heart, pour each out-breath out from the heart.

Start with your own misery, feel it with as much intensity as possible: the hurt, the wounds, and the suffering in your whole life. Accept it and welcome it. Breathe in your own misery ... absorb it into the heart. Let it be transformed there into joy, into bliss. Breathe out all the joy, the blissfulness, pour yourself into existence.

Now expand this process. Take the whole misery of all beings, unconditionally, friends, enemies, family, strangers. Accept and welcome it. Breathe in all the misery and hell ... absorb it into the heart. Let it be transformed there into joy, into bliss. Breathe out all the joy, the blissfulness, pour yourself into existence.

Now completely withdraw your attention from the world, from others, even from yourself. Enjoy being silent and still.

EXERCISE #6:
The Quickest Route to Tantric Sex

Tantra is about making love into an art. If you thought of yourself as an artist of love, what would you create? If you were painting a picture of the most juicy, delicious, perfect afternoon with your beloved, composing a song, or sculpting a masterpiece, how would you honor them?

Tantric lovers take their time. They are not in a hurry. Tantra has everything to do with savoring the moment, and bringing awareness to every detail. Noticing what you've never noticed before. Did you ever consider that the inside of the elbow could be an erogenous zone? That you can turn on your partner by tickling the small of his or her back?

The quickest route to tantric sex is to slow down, waaaay down. Do everything you normally do, but twice or even three times slower than usual. Focus first on anything and everything but the genitals. Slow. Slowly. Uhmmmm, painfully, agonizingly slow.

As leisurely as you've ever touched anyone, stroke down the inside of their thigh in the most languorous motion possible. Brush their nipples with your palm with a touch as light as a peacock feather. Your hand slides down their side so slowly that its movement would be imperceptible to an observer, as if you weren't even moving. When you take as much time as you've ever wanted to lick, swirl, and savor, the taste of our beloved's lips is divine. Pleasure him or her with the slow Chinese water torture of your touch.

Think of your gratitude for this moment, for your lover, for being able to express your celebration through your hands. Each moment is precious and sacred if you only pay attention. Be meditative, intimate; prolong the act of love.

Sting once told reporters that he and his wife, Trudie, practiced tantric sex for up to four hours at a time. He later explained that this time frame included their flirtation, having dinner, getting undressed, and sexual play, all as a part of tantric lovemaking. In tantra, these activities are not seen as "foreplay," but rather as opportunities for awareness and sexual pleasure; they are not less than intercourse itself.

Even if you think you are bored with this partner, with their body, approach it as if you've never been with it before. Watch with your awareness how much you can learn about pleasing a body you thought you knew. Enjoy your lover responding in ways you've never experienced before. How could anyone ever not be in the mood if every time were exquisitely different, shimmering with awareness? In tantric lovemaking, the quickest route is the slowest.

Tantric Relating

Relationship Advice to Find and
Keep Sex, Love and Romance

Tantric Relating
INTRODUCTION

We relate differently when the Other is the Beloved.

Compare: In contemporary culture, the other person is frequently seen as an enemy or someone to compete with or be jealous of. The other is someone you can't trust and must play skillful games with if you want to get ahead. You've studied ways to improve communication because you're into personal and spiritual growth, but you haven't found what's out there as helpful as you hoped because, as in conventional dating and mating, the underlying premise beneath the conventional worldview will never work. Tantra offers the antidote to all this dis-ease, a radical perspective on relating.

With all the talking going on out there it seems as if we must be relating, but our results show otherwise. With over half of all relationships calling it quits, with nations and tribes at war, and with simple civility toward our fellow humans taking a nosedive—perhaps the way we are relating is contributing to a crisis in communication rather than making things better.

As a person serious about personal and spiritual growth, you may have experienced relating as a major challenge—it is for most people. You may have felt that you were talking too much or too little, that you need to keep who you are hidden away, concealing the extent of your hopes and dreams, or that you were being too bold or too shy. This confusion showed up in your romantic life as secrets, lots of crying, broken trust, and in the end, the death of the coupledom. You kept reading self-help books and online articles, but rapport with would-be partners spiraled quickly downward.

You've most likely tried being a positive, upbeat person, not sharing things that your partner might not like. You've even experimented with mind-reading and subterfuge. You've kept your opinions and unhappiness to yourself, or shared them only with your therapist and friends. The fights and blowups inexplicably continued.

As a Licensed Marriage and Family Therapist working with individuals and couples, I've noticed that conventional suggestions for improving communication don't help much. Active listening, still prescribed by therapists and coaches, has been scientifically proven not to work (cited in Gottman, see notes). Scheduling special times to talk, practicing positivity, writing down criticisms, women speaking in different ways than men—when we remember to do these actions they might help, but when we forget, things get worse; and they're hard to remember in the heat of things. These conventional techniques, while well-intended, do not stem the bleeding.

It was the tantric perspective that changed everything for me, as it was in dating and mating. In tantra, everything is perfect in this moment, so what is true in the present is welcome, even if it's hard. It's also the tantric perspective that whoever is in front of you in this moment is the Beloved, your chance to experience love or not, and that it is up to you, not the other person.

I didn't understand the extent to which conventional ideas about relating were having a negative effect on my relationships until I met my Perfect Beloved, now husband, Greg Lawrence. Greg had experienced the devastation of conventional relating in his previous partnerships, and he was craving something different this time. Together, we pieced out what we wanted for our partnership, and it has been working so well that we can honestly say that our relationship is light-years beyond what we ever imagined for ourselves.

I don't think it's on anyone's relationship goals list to sit and stew in silence, or to experience those excruciating conversational log jams. We all long for someone with whom we can talk freely and have our ideas and enthusiasms warmly received. We crave living in an atmosphere of total trust and safety, and to luxuriate in a frequency of love and support. And what about the world of non-verbal communication? In tantra we are all about the body, so that must be addressed as well.

This book, *Tantric Relating*, is about how you can communicate both verbally and non- to keep the love fires burning, and to find and keep the sex, love and romance of your dreams. In *Tantric Dating*, the secrets of why you haven't found love and how to find it are explained. *Tantric Mating* illuminates how to be in partnership and create your perfect soulmate relationship. In this book, you'll learn how to make agreements about truth sharing, how to know when an issue is resolved, how and why to clear all resentments, how to praise, thank and flirt, and why "When in doubt, touch."

The teachings in this book can change all your relationships, not just the one with your Beloved. Yes, you can use these principles to create the love affair of your dreams. After that, or while you're waiting, please join us in applying them widely to help the world blossom into an oasis of love.

TANTRIC RELATING MINDSET

To Tell the Truth or Not, That Is the Question

We're taught from an early age not to speak our truth. We'll get in trouble if we do, or we'll be spanked, shamed, or isolated. We learn to sit quietly and behave. Of course, it's good not to let children run around screaming in restaurants or tell Uncle Joe that he smells funny, so part of this shaping of personalities is mastering how to coexist with other people. However, the brainwashing has begun: it's not safe to speak your truth.

Girls are socialized to not offer our opinions in class, to not appear too smart, and to always act in a pleasing manner. Boys are brainwashed to never feel or express feelings, including not crying, and to appear as though they don't give a damn. Of course, if you don't identify as strictly male or female you are SOL. People of color are expected to adopt the dominant worldview without complaint, and old people, well, old people should just shut up and fade away.

In the workplace, even though many bosses state they want an open environment where people can speak freely, only the most naive would take them at their word. The modern dating market is rife with "expert" advice on how to tangle one's words around to manipulate others into desiring us. Most of us have no idea how much we've been hypnotized to accept the mainstream's version of us as ourselves, or how to find or locate our personal truth.

It's good that we learn how to conform and not share too much of our personal selves in the social and work spheres. If we want to be successful, these are necessary skills. However, in intimate partnerships, the opposite is true. The problem is that people get into love relationships with no understanding that speaking their own truth and being open to the truth of their partner(s) is what creates intimacy and connection.

With all this training to NOT tell the truth about ourselves, how are we supposed to suddenly BE our true selves in relationships?

Humming along underneath all this socialization and programming of how to be successful in the world is the heartbeat of tantra. Tantra teaches us that everything is perfect in the present moment; therefore, whatever your or your partner's personal truth is is part of that perfection, even if it creates difficulty. You would want to express your truth, and you would want your partner to express their truth. In tantra, everything is divine, so every feeling that you have and share with your partner would be divine as well.

When you enter into a relationship inspired by tantric principles, you and your partner will be encouraged to share your complete and honest truth with each other. You'll see: it makes for great sex and intimacy.

Permission to Be Unkind

We all say things we wish we hadn't. Maybe you were a little more curt or not as caring as you would like to have been. Perhaps you realize you've been sarcastic or cutting. Sometimes you don't realize your part until later when you're wondering how that fight began. Relating does not go as hoped often due to our human frailties, so when it's been with a person you're close to, it's good to check in and see, "Is that something I'd say to my boss, coworker, or friend?" If it's not, it's important to admit that you gave yourself permission to be unkind.

This is normally when someone responds, "Well, I couldn't help it," or "I was all stressed out," or "The other person was being a @%#&." The fact is, nearly everyone has the ability to not make out-of-control comments to people in authority. You would take care to never talk rudely to your boss, for example. You edit yourself for police and in social situations, so this idea that "I couldn't help it" really doesn't hold weight.

Becoming aware of and getting over giving ourselves permission to be unkind is an inside job. It's not about the other person and that what they've done is irritating or triggering. It's about "Do I want to grow myself up so I'm not a person who gives myself permission to say unkind things?" You make an internal decision to raise your own standards of behavior. You want to take responsibility so that these mean statements don't stick and have a permanent effect on your relationship, and the other person isn't injured because you spouted off.

There are certain things that only an intimate partnership brings up. You may have been working on yourself diligently, but as soon as you enter a relationship, boom, your neglected inner child comes out. Sometimes because of our unresolved past, we might feel like letting ourselves go and acting like a two-year-old. This may be a challenge, especially if you grew up in a sometimes unkind home, but it's worth the effort to change because you become a person who never speaks hurtfully.

There's the added fact that when you let yourself go and say inconsiderate things, terrible self-esteem follows, and in a way that's right because why should we feel good about less-than-loving behavior? It's time to remind yourself that even if you're not perfect, you're working earnestly at becoming as kind and compassionate as you aspire to be. This kind of personal work is advantageous for you, your partner, your relationship, and the greater community. The whole world benefits from kind, evolving individuals and happy couples.

Don't Rock the Boat, Baby

"Rock the Boat" was the name of a worldwide disco hit back in the '70s. The infectious chorus repeated, "Rock the boat, don't rock the boat, baby," over and over. It's said that every minute of the day that song is playing somewhere in the world. A friend of mine's uncle wrote it, and apparently, he lived high all his life on the royalties from that one song.

A fun song but maybe not the best relationship advice. Another issue that can sink the ship of relationships is that "Don't rock the boat" is a strategy many couples use as they attempt to navigate their relating: Don't talk about that difficult thing! It'll create more trouble! You're not supposed to talk about stuff like that. Don't rock the boat because it will make your partner unhappy. You smile, say nothing's wrong when it obviously is, and refuse to discuss the thing that's bugging you.

You may have the best intentions, but all that unspoken communication begins to pile up and create congestion on the high seas. The problems don't go away; in fact, they multiply because nothing is getting solved. It shows up in the bedroom as "I'm not in the mood." Yes, it's difficult to bring up the topic that our sex life has gotten stale, but do you think your partner hasn't noticed?

If you or your partner are arguing a lot, or are not using loving language, don't you think both of you are unhappy? Yes, there are many things you can bring up that are going to make your partner uncomfortable, but that is part of how we grow.

A commonly used metaphor is that each person in a relationship is wearing a backpack, and everything that doesn't get discussed is a rock that gets stored back there. Little by little as rocks keep being added with each topic not discussed, the load gets heavier and heavier until one day, one person throws the contents of their backpack out on the table, and all hell breaks loose.

Juicy, alive relationships require having their boat rocked. Unless you want to end up as one of those couples sitting in restaurants not talking to each other, bored with life, you'll need to share what's going on with you, getting into complete agreement and honesty. Honesty sometimes leads to difficulty. Part of tantric relating is making agreements with your partner that you *will* rock the boat. Anything that's not talked about is going to eventually cause holes in your boat and make it impossible for you to have the rich, juicy sex, love and romance that your soul longs for.

The Spiritual Path of Relating

If you realized that the person sitting in front of you was your Beloved, how would you treat them? I suspect it would be with kindness and love. You would focus on their strengths and good points and ignore what you perceive to be the less-so. (After all, that's how we treat our friends, right?) You'd speak carefully and tenderly and attend to their comfort. You'd feel grateful that love has shown up for you and count your blessings. And maybe, just maybe, you'd be aware of the divine spark at the core of that other person's being, silently blazing away, equal to the one inside you.

But, your mind says, this person isn't flawless enough to be my perfect partner. This person is—fill in the blank—not good looking enough, they've gained weight, they're too messy or too much of a neatnik, they don't have sex as often or as little as you do and when they do it's not the right way to get you off. If you observe carefully, you'll notice that your mind wants to itemize every "wrong" thing about this person as an explanation for why they aren't your perfect love. The mind doesn't like the idea that anyone but a fantasy figure is the Beloved, so it rejects the real human being and closes your heart.

You've been taught by the conventional culture that love exists sometime in the future when you'll meet and get involved with a perfect person, or that love is only to be given to people who look and act a certain way. In tantra, we learn that if we can't relate to the person in front of us with love and awareness, we won't be available for love with our romantic partner either.

Early in my work with one of my mentors, he told me that he relates to a homeless person on a bench the same way he treats a fashion model. Most of us would treat one of those people with derision and disrespect and the other with adulation and fawning behavior. At that moment my mentor's near-sainthood in relating to other beings became clear to me, and I have forever more aspired to that level of respect and tantric relating.

An elevating ideal, perhaps, but difficult in practice? Yes, but worth pursuing as we turn ourselves into lovers. When we practice relating to everyone as an emanation of the divine, we gain skill in the art of relating to our partner. Tantra is about seeing sex, love and romance as part of the spiritual path, and everyone we encounter is an opportunity for practice.

The first step in tantric relating is that relating to others becomes an essential element of your spiritual path, one of the major avenues for expressing our love in the world. All little moments between you and another are opportunities to practice becoming a more loving person. Every encounter with another is an encounter with the divine.

You can begin today relating in the tantric way by realizing that whomever you are with right now is a divine being, and it is up to you to recognize it. Relate to everyone as someone you love, most not in the romantic sense, but in a spirit of camaraderie as spiritual brothers and sisters helping each other grow. The more you practice with everyone you meet, the more your heart will open and become accustomed to sharing love in every moment.

Relating Through the Body

Tantra is all about being in the body. Conventional culture insists we live our lives in our heads: thinking, analyzing, judging. Most of us don't even like our bodies very much. We've been taught (relentlessly) by social media and advertising that our bodies are not shaped right, and that we need to aspire to be different. Our bodies may carry memories of past trauma we'd like to forget. We've become more comfortable watching life with our eyes and brains, instead of participating in the often-messy IRL.

Most of us have no idea that we're not IN our bodies. It wasn't until I lived at the tantra ashram that I learned there was another way. I had always assumed I was in my body because I was a dancer, did yoga, and ate healthy, but at the ashram I learned that these were things I was doing TO my body. Not that there's anything wrong with trying to be healthy and fit, but I had never asked my body if these were routines it wanted or enjoyed. I'd been forcing disciplines on it, some of which in the long run turned out to be unhealthy.

When we relate tantrically, we acknowledge that we live in bodies. Not the perfect, airbrushed online images, but living, breathing, conscious bodies. Bodies that don't always smell good or do what we want them to. When your body's enlivened by practicing embodiment exercises and awareness practices, you become attentive to the fact that your physical self is never not communicating. The body is sharing your aliveness, or enthusiasm, or lack of sleep. It communicates its delicious desire, or fear or blockages. You become willing to learn from its wisdom.

Tantric relating is through the fingertips, the breath, the sounds, and the soul. Psychologists say that only 7 percent of communication is verbal. If you live in your head you miss most of what is being related. What is your body saying? What does a hand on your shoulder mean, or a kiss on the forehead? Arms folded protecting the heart? What do you communicate about respect for the other person when you ask permission before giving a hug?

Our bodies long for touch. You might even feel touch starved—no shame there—many people if not most, do. Often reaching out and sharing touch speaks way more than words. When you're embodied and relate through the physical, are not ashamed of your body, comfortable with expressing physical affection, your vibe will be one of love.

Clear, open tantric relating will be enhanced when we clear our shame about our bodies, past abuse, fears about being touched, loved, being intimate. Fears that we love too much, that the other person will leave us or laugh at us, that our love will not be reciprocated. When you work with and move past these fears you'll be able to touch without shame, fear, embarrassment, or concern about sexual performance.

If you are deeply relating to your own body, you will be open and excited to communicate with your lover's body. Bodies by themselves, when cleared of mental chatter and resentments, want to make love, and they don't want to stop. One person with a healed body meets another person with a healed body: this is one of the elements that contributes to tantric sex being as good as you've heard it is.

Agreements to Talk about Everything

One of the reasons we choose to relate differently in a tantric relationship is because we want to keep the energy clear between us. Only then can we have beautiful tantric sex, because only then can we exist in a blissful climate free of resentments, anger, and fights. If you are mad at your partner, unhappy with them, or in a snit, you will be unhappy in your life and your lovemaking, if it exists at all, will be unsatisfying. To say the least.

Making an agreement to talk about everything creates a safe ambiance, strengthening the climate of trust in your relationship so that you won't ever have to worry that your partner is keeping something from you. To agree to talk about everything means you know you can speak your mind and the other person isn't going to freak out, accuse you of misdeeds, or call you names.

In previous relationships, there were probably many things you couldn't talk about. For example, you didn't know for certain how your partner was feeling but it felt risky to ask, or they would just answer "fine" when you knew they weren't. You had a gut feeling they weren't happy, but they wouldn't talk about it so you weren't sure. You suspected they were flirting with other people on social media; perhaps it turned out to be true. But you weren't able to bring these things up, because it seemed better to keep from rocking the boat.

In a relationship where an agreement has been made to talk about everything, you would already have permission to ask, "Hey, how are you feeling?" or "Are you less happy with our relationship than you used to be? How would you like us to change?" And your partner would feel free to answer, "Yes, I'd like more physical affection. Seems like we used to have that more, and I miss it." Whatever the truth might be, you can talk about it. The issues are out in the open and don't have to be hidden, hitting you unsuspectingly when they come to light.

I saw a patient the other day who was trying to express what he wanted to do on vacation, and his partner called him a snob for his desire to spend the night at an expensive resort. Being put down like that obviously doesn't help the conversation move forward. This name-calling made it unsafe for him to bring up his wants and desires for fear of being ridiculed.

Having an agreement to talk about everything also means conversations may get difficult sometimes. In tantra, since the entire world is held as sacred, every emotion would be sacred too. There is nothing that would not be, so we would welcome difficult feelings, arguments, misunderstandings—all are part of our personal and spiritual growth. Living with an agreement to talk about everything will be worth any challenges because of the great freedom it creates, the freedom to bring your full self to the relationship so you can be truly loved as you are.

Thus one of the foundational steps in tantric relating is to have a conversation with your partner about whether or not you want to make such an agreement. How much truth do you want to share? How much freedom do you and your partner want to live in? Are you willing to hear their truth? Make your version of the agreement together—even daring to have the discussion will evolve your relationship to new depth.

The Process of Clearing

Everything you haven't talked about is going to show up in the bedroom. It's bound to appear as "I don't feel like it" or "I'm not in the mood" or you wondering why three months have gone by since the two of you made love. When you're carrying a grudge, even if it's over something tiny and supposedly insignificant, you won't feel like getting intimate. And who can blame you?

That's why it's important, if you want great relating and a great sex life, to have an agreement not only to talk about everything, but also to clear things as soon as you're aware there's an issue. What does that mean? Here's an example:

You're taking a morning walk together, and you notice you're feeling a tad uncomfortable.

Instead of ignoring it, you look inside and assess that you're anxious because your partner said something sharply at breakfast, and you've felt a bit miffed ever since. So, with the permission to bring things up, you would ask, "May I bring something up?" (It's always a good idea to make sure this is a good time so as to not ambush them.) "I'm still not done about the disagreement we had this morning. I felt you spoke to me in a harsh way that wasn't justified. Do you feel I am overreacting?"

And your partner might reply, "Oh, no, sorry. I was a tired and, I guess, grumpy. I was thinking about something I read in the news that triggered me, so no, I'm not upset with you. Thanks for asking."

Right there, you're not going home all worried that they're mad at you, or that you said something stupid. You know how the mind can go on and on that maybe what you said ruined things. The monkey mind can create all kinds of scenarios to torture us if we don't stop in the moment and check things out with the other person.

You may have had previous relationships where the smallest thing would trigger World War III. If you don't bring issues up, little blips of resentment expand and multiply and before you know it, someone leaves the refrigerator door open and there's a huge skirmish that has nothing to do with the fridge—it's about all the minor issues that have built up over time. So, if you don't want that type of relating, you'll get to the point where you'll be happy to bring things up, because you don't want to be carrying them forward, affecting your mood, your motivation level, a lack of emotional comfort, or whether or not you feel secure in your relationship.

Firstly, agree to bring things up to be cleared. Secondly, discuss as soon as possible, although later is better than never. Lastly, talk about whatever is between you until both people feel satisfied. When you clear things in the moment, perfect love reappears. You've returned to that lovely river of energy that connects you. That's always the goal, to get back to that pure stream of love, flowing like water.

Clearing the Past

Many couples' relationships are trapped in layers of resentment. The lovers are still unfinished or mad about things that happened a year ago, five years ago, maybe even twenty depending on the length of the relationship. When a couple has gotten into trouble or is not making love any more, there's usually much excavating of the past that needs to be done in order to thrive together in the present moment.

Spiritual traditions have a long history of methods for an individual to clear their past. For example, in Toltec shamanism, there's a process in which you list every incident that has happened in your life and then clear and clean it. Twelve-step programs include the Fourth Step where you make a list of everyone you've felt resentment toward in your life, you take responsibility for your part in the upset, and then release it by sharing with a trusted advisor. In another tradition, the process is called *clearing*, where you go back to everything in the past that still has "charge" on it. The results of this clearing process are actually read on a meter to measure whether or not your issue is complete. Psychotherapy attempts to clear traumatic incidents in the past that are still causing distress.

What does this mean that you clear the past until you don't "have charge on it" anymore? It means: If your body is still responding to the memory of the event, you are not done. Do you still cry, does your breath stop, do feelings come up into your heart or make you feel sick to your stomach? These are all indications that the issue has not been cleared. In your work on yourself as an individual, you process these memories until there's no more upset about anything from your past. Anything that's not clear, anything you're still afraid or ashamed of, anything that you've not forgiven yourself for or feel sad about will show up not only in not having the best life possible, but also as challenges in your relationships.

For couples this means going back and clearing all memories of upset, which can be a lengthy process. Every incident from the past that hasn't been cleared is going to show up as difficulty in the present moment. If there are still resentments, it's going to show up in the bedroom.

It's an archaeological excavation, rooting these things out, talking them through until neither of you is upset about them anymore. You may benefit from the assistance of a therapist or coach.

Even doing a little bit of this work will help. It's possible, however, to actually be completely cleared of the past, and if you stick with the process for that long, a metaphysical shift happens. A clarity, a freshness, an in-rush of energy takes the place of all that had been previously muddying the water. It's a phenomenal thing. It's within reach for you as a couple to bring this to completion. Then as you continue to clear on a daily basis, nothing piles up anymore. To be in that clear of a space with your Beloved is worth all the effort it took to get there.

Thank You for Bringing That Up

If you're going to have an agreement to bring everything up, you and your partner will most probably need to cultivate a changed attitude from the one you have now. Doing this practice, you're bound to learn things about yourself that are tough to hear. You were thinking you were being cool, but listening to your partner's point of view, you have to admit that, yes, you were instead being moody and a tad unkind. This comes as a ding to the ego. You're not as together as you thought, but really, isn't that the point? To grow out of having bad moods and taking them out on people? It often hurts when the truth's brought up—sometimes it's a pinprick; other times it pierces the heart.

Saying "Thank you for bringing that up," when our partner shares their truth, especially when it's difficult to hear, is a practice that will bypass the ego's interference. In that one phrase you are not only reinforcing to yourself that you want to hear things, even if they're difficult, so you can grow, but also acknowledging your partner's risk at sharing their truth, and that you welcome them doing so now and in the future.

"Thank you for bringing that up." Sometimes it will hurt to say that. Maybe during a conflict you got offended, and your ego doesn't feel particularly grateful. In that moment, if you thank your partner for bringing things up with you instead of withholding, you're going to feel better. Sometimes you have to push yourself over that hill when you feel a little resentment. Remember your commitment to personal and spiritual growth.

Tantric relating grows through this process. When someone brings something up you did, you should be willing to examine your part in it, as it may be a pointer to how you need to mature and where you need to change. You might suddenly see a lifetime of conditioning, something you've been doing for twenty or thirty years—it isn't the way you want to be and you shouldn't be doing it any more.

This process clears the throat chakra, which is clogged from all the things we've never said, all the things it wasn't safe to say. When you're tantric relating, speaking truth and having your truth received, talking through everything, then everything you have to say with each other creates safety in your relationship.

Making agreements and thanking the other person for honoring them keeps the frequency between you clear and vitally alive. If instead you're cringing at the thought of what they might say, or they are hoping you won't bring things up, you're never going to get to the space of pure, vibrating clarity. Try it and you'll agree—it's the fast track of relating.

Really, Until It's Done

You've made agreements to talk about things when they happen, or at least as soon as possible. You know that by letting misunderstandings fester, you run the risk of them mutating into something else altogether. Often, however, in your zeal to be happy, you will prematurely agree that an issue has been completely talked out. You nod, say everything's okay, and go on your merry way. Except that later in the day you find yourself being cranky, or you don't feel in the mood to make love, or find yourself sniping and angry. That's a sign that you're not done with everything that needed to be said. Sometimes talking about things until they're done may take a while.

Early on, I had an experience where something Greg said triggered me, and I realized I still had unfinished business from a year ago. I felt a little defensive bringing up an issue after so much time had passed, but since we have an agreement to talk about everything until it's done, that's what we did. It took several conversations for both of us to feel entirely clear, and when it was really done, it was like seeing the sun after a grim morning gloom.

In this example, if you had asked us, we would have both said the incident was done, but when I looked deeply, I could see that I still had charge that needed to be cleared. If it's not done for one person, it's not done for either of you. You can't be at the same frequency if one of you is holding on to something, no matter how miniscule or far in the past.

You might find that you and/or your partner are quick to want to declare something resolved, because it's uncomfortable not being done and you want to move on. That's understandable. This is also referred to as "sweeping things under the carpet" or "don't rock the boat." If and when you prematurely announce something complete, there remains a barely perceptible sensation that something's not quite right, which shows up as feeling distant from your partner. It decreases your desire for intimacy.

Sometimes you have to remind your partner, "Remember how we have an agreement to talk about everything until it's done? I want to bring up something. Is this a good time?" It's not always going to be pretty. Neither of you might want to get into a debate or be in the mood to dredge up old painful memories; you might find it triggering. Your partner might respond, "Really? Do you have to bring this up now? Aren't you done with that yet?" By focusing on the outcome—the energy clear and flowing freely between you—you become willing to do the work in order to make things better. The agreement is that you will continue until each person is done. Really done.

To make sure you're really done, another thing you can do to make space for the other person is to ask them, "What else? Are you sure, is there anything more? It feels like you're not quite done." You open yourself to receive your partner's truth, even if it stings.

How will you know when something's finished? Because you're making love beautifully. There's no sniping. You're both free to talk about whatever; you're having fun. That's how you know the communication's clear. If it's not, something's clogging the pipes, and it's up to you to unblock the line. The learning curve can be steep, but once you learn to feel the energy and clear anything that's in the space between you, you will love the feeling. After that, it comes easily and becomes the only way to live, in complete clarity and in the present moment. Tantric relating is when the two of you are completely free and open with no unfinished business between you.

Space to Be Upset

Tantric relating teaches us to give another person space to be upset. Women especially have been socialized to be so codependent that we rush in and try to fix our partner's feelings before they've even had a chance to feel them. Your partner's unhappiness can be so distressing to you that you try all kinds of strategies: denial that anything is wrong, premature forgiveness, or shaming them for having feelings at all. "That shouldn't bother you!"

In order to relate tantrically in a way that supports a soulmate relationship, you'll need to allow your partner their space to be upset, without interference. This can be difficult especially if you've come from a challenging childhood and aren't yet able to count on secure love, but practicing it will build strength in you and your partnership. If your partner's unsettled they have a right to their feelings. They deserve to deal with their inner experience alone and separate from you. I admit it can feel threatening.

Let me give you an example. Greg and I stopped by the Ventura County Fair on our way home from a day of sightseeing and were entering the grounds from the parking lot.

Greg reported, "Something triggered me and I was instantly in a bad mood. I didn't want to talk. I wanted to be pissed off. Catherine said something like, 'It's a nice day. I'm glad we're here.' I don't know why it did, but that bugged me. It seemed she barely knew that I was upset.

"I think I was in the porta potty when I came to my senses, and I said to myself, 'What the hell am I doing? This is a nice day. I do not want to be upset.' I pulled myself together and went back to her and I said, 'Wow, that was really bad. I'm sorry.' She said, 'That's okay. I knew you'd be back.'"

This example shows how if you're able to not take it personally and just wait a little while, the other person often gets ahold of themselves. You give them their space to return to the loving, independent person you know them to be.

Someone really wise once defined a successful relationship as one where only one person is crazy at a time. This means that occasionally you'll have to stand up and be the "sane one" because your partner is emotional and not at their best. You rise up as a rock of support for them. If the other person's momentarily unhinged and you know it's not because of anything you've said or done, you can give them their space, trusting that they'll return to you later. It helps to know that another person is holding space for you to be upset, and will be there for you when you come back to yourself.

Praise, Thanks, and Flirting

Who in the world has ever said, "Please stop saying nice things about me. I've had enough"? No one. Who doesn't like to receive praise? In relationships, partners have often gotten into a habit of pointing out what's "wrong" with the other person: what we don't like and how they're not living up to our expectations, often communicated in a subtly disguised "just being helpful."

John and Julie Gottman, the psychologists who hook people up to electrodes and measure what actually works, found that in relationships between happy couples, the individuals are saying nice things to each other five times to the one time they have some sort of criticism. Every time you say, "Could you please clean up a bit more after yourself in the kitchen?" there will need to be five incidents of praise. Five to one!

This is a math equation few of us make use of, but it's something that can begin improving your relationship(s) immediately. Consciously remembering to make positive statements raises everyone's mood. Here are three action steps to get started on right away, and best of all—they're fun!

Praise

When you're busy looking for things to praise about your partner, it's easy once you get going. You can praise their appearance: "You look hot in those pants." You can admire how they handle things: "The way you talked with Charlie was so powerful. I was proud of you." There are their achievements at work, that they stay fit, and their kindness with people. There's the all-purpose "I love you; you're awesome." How many more can you come up with?

Thanks

Thanks and showing appreciation makes people feel good, both the one giving the thanks and the one receiving. Certainly in the outside world we hear that we don't make much of a difference. To come home to a warm nest where our partner is praising and thanking us is part of creating a soulmate relationship.

You can thank your partner for being in your life, for showing up and being a good person. "Thank you for taking the garbage out. I really appreciate it." "Thanks for taking care of our family." Greg and I thank each other for our morning exercise: "Thanks for taking that walk with me." We even thank each other after we have sex: "Thank you. That was so beautiful." How often do you express your gratitude?

Flirting

You may have had effective flirting skills when you were dating, but like most people, have forgotten to exercise them after you've been with someone for a while. Maybe you think it's not so easy to flirt when you've been hanging out together on the couch in your joggers, exchanged morning breath, and had more than a few spats. That's conventional thinking, and prone to make you blame your partner for why you're not making love any more.

If you want sex in your relationship, you'll want to remember to acknowledge your partner's sexiness. The best definition I've heard of flirting is that it's letting the other person know you see their sex appeal, especially if you're not going to act on it. It doesn't mean you're going to have sex now or later. It could—it's always fun to have the possibility hanging in the air. You make an acknowledgment of the other person's attractiveness in some cute way, a fun way, or even just through your energy.

If you're not going to praise, thank and flirt with your partner, who is? Answer: someone else, or no one. If your partner is going to get enough love in this lifetime, don't you want to be the one to provide it? You want them to be radiantly happy and to acknowledge that they're in their dream relationship. These small, easy-to-do actions go a very long way.

When in Doubt, Touch

Touch is all-important for tantric relating. Tantrikas practice reminding ourselves that we live in bodies not just our heads, and that we want to relate to our Beloved from an embodied awareness not just from our minds analyzing everything. A mind in full-bore analysis mode can destroy even the best relationship. Nonverbal communication and touch speak louder than words.

It's true that we need to make agreements to talk about everything and continue the conversation until it's done. Yet sometimes you get stuck and the discussion is spiraling downward, and you don't know how to make it stop. At these times it's good to take a time-out and return later to finish. It's good for your bodies to connect for a few moments, placing a hand on the other's knee or arm as a way to communicate wordlessly, "I care for you. I know we're having trouble right now, but I want to work this out."

Your bodies will remember your connection even if you don't. For a moment, you won't be lost in your head arguing, coming up with points to make your case. When you settle into your body and reconnect in a friendly, loving way, your anxiety will lessen and your breath will slow down. Put your hand on their shoulder or arm, and simply connect. This will help the conversation veer away from two egos fighting to "Hey, we're a couple. We're going through this together. Let's breathe and let our bodies communicate." A simple gesture like this can often help guide the two of you out of the most difficult situations.

There's a great book called *How to Improve Your Marriage Without Talking About It* by Dr. Patricia Love. I once saw her speak, and she's quite charismatic and dynamic. The book isn't essential reading, but it does offer actual scientific studies that show that sometimes if you're in a difficult place in your relationship, if you will just reach out and reconnect with the other person through touch, the conversation will become easier. This is quite profound and useful information.

Bodies are often smarter than we are. When you get in a stuck space with your Beloved, touch. When you want to express affection, touch. When you want to offer support, congratulations, or difficult news, connect through gentle physical contact. Whenever you're in doubt about what to do, share your love through the gift of your touch.

Relating Romantically

Conventional culture offers tried-and-true symbols to message that you're seeking romance: candles, flowers, low lighting, soft music, chocolates, delightful scents, delicious bites of forbidden food. All these things communicate "I'm wanting to relate romantically," and a tantric lover will make liberal use of them.

As a society, we've agreed that some places are more romantic than others. We usually imagine taking a stroll by the beach together, often at sunset. We picture dimly lit cafes serving French food and wine. Each couple will designate other locales as romantic depending on their histories, but one thing we all agree on is that the bedroom is a prime place for love, sex and romance. To relate romantically, you want to invest time and energy to make your bedroom beautiful. Once when I was talking about this on a podcast, the host said, "I'm going to go home and take the work papers out of the bedroom." That's a good idea! You want to create a dream space for romantic intimacy.

Romantic relating is also expressed nonverbally through slow, sensuous touch. You create a cocoon of safety for your partner: You can trust me; I will not make fun of you. You cuddle up together offering nurturing and softness. Romantic intimacy has to do with "I love the way you express yourself; I love your sexual expression." You communicate through your open heart, through loving touch.

Romantic relating also involves sexuality. We're looking for passion. We want to feel our energies rise. When we think of romantic ways of expressing sexuality, it most often is soft and slow and may take hours. At other times we may prefer lust and quickies, but for romance we want to gaze into our lover's eyes and take our time.

You want to consider not only what we as a culture agree on as romantic symbols, signs, and gestures. You also want to meditate on what puts you in the mood. What reminds you that your relationship is special and unique? Remember when you two were first in love—you felt as if no one's ever been in love as much as this. Wrap that silky blanket around you. Share memories from those early days. Help each other get into a space of romantic intimacy: We are a special couple; we are special to each other. You want to have a sense of your own power—you can create romantic intimacy.

The Sky's the Limit

A relationship is never going to be a finished commodity if you stay alive and growing. It's true that familiarity can make things seem stale, and either of you could go to sleep. When we saw those types of relationships as kids or as singles, fear loomed in us that we might end up like that. I doubt anybody dreams of a relationship that's going downhill. Make a commitment that you're going to grow, and really go for it.

Whether or not your relationship stays vibrant will depend on your commitment to relate to each other as manifestations of the divine. It is contingent on agreeing to talk about everything, and being a big enough person to listen to ways you've been unkind or hurtful. It's an essential component of enlightened relating to bring things up right away, when they happen, and to talk about them until they're done. As you continue to grow, you'll become increasingly sensitive to the state of the energy between you and your partner. You'll find you'll want to clear everything current and past because even the slightest being "out" feels unbearable.

Osho said we have until our last breath to continue to grow and evolve. That can be the same with your relationship, that your relationship will continue to evolve, becoming more loving, kinder, more generous, less reactive, and less judgmental. It can also get juicier, sexier, and more alive as we get older. That can be your reality if you choose it. You can, in the same way as you made a commitment to your own growth, make a commitment to the growth of your relationship.

What we are advocating in this book is keeping the space between yourself and another person clear. Sometimes this will mean working through difficult stuff—sadness, resentment, jealousy, insecurity—in tantra we view it all as divine.

Allowing the feelings to come up and sharing them in a way that creates more trust, until the process is done. Living in our bodies and sharing our healing touch. Remembering how amazing it is that this person has chosen to be in partnership with us (for whatever length of time) and expressing our gratitude frequently. Living these practices will show up in lovemaking where there's nothing in the way, the bodily expression of love flowing freely.

In *Tantric Dating*, the secrets of why you haven't found love and how to find it are explained. *Tantric Mating* teaches how to be in partnership and create your perfect soulmate relationship. This book, *Tantric Relating*, has been about how you can communicate both verbally and non- to keep the love fires burning.

If you both have the desire to grow personally and spiritually as much as you can in this lifetime, you'll someday arrive at the place where you find you've created the intimate relationship of your dreams. This is possible for you. I wholeheartedly want to encourage you to keep working on your personal and spiritual growth because perfect love is possible for you—the sky's the limit.

TANTRIC RELATING EXERCISES

EXERCISE #1:
Envisioning Your Lover as the God or Goddess They Truly Are

One tantric exercise you can practice at home is to envision your lover as the god or goddess they truly are. That may seem a bit farfetched in today's world, as modern lovers are all too aware of what is "wrong" with their partner. Constantly bombarded with images of what the perfect lover looks like, talks like, kisses like, and makes love like, we compare and analyze and find our partners not measuring up. Since it is hard for a mere human being to live up to these two-dimensional fantasy figures, most of us experience our lovers (and ourselves) as lacking in the love department.

But what if we didn't focus on what we thought was wrong, but on what is right? What if we imagined the real person underneath their skin and their annoying habits? What if we pictured our

Beloved as their essential nature and allowed ourselves to honor their lovingness, their vulnerability, and their attempts at becoming a better person?

When we imagine our partner as whole and perfect instead of fragmented and flawed, it becomes impossible to abuse, degrade, or dehumanize the other person. If they are by definition an equal, we cannot cultivate a condescending, contemptuous attitude. On the contrary, we view them with the gaze of a deity who is one of tenderness, clarity, and passion. Seeing our self as whole and perfect, our partner becomes a mirror of that perfection.

Ancient Tantric Buddhists practiced seeing the man as a male Buddha and the woman as a female Buddha, and therefore, lovemaking became two Buddhas making love. The lovers practiced seeing each other as pure energy spontaneously expressing itself in embodied being.

Today, you can have fun with these practices. Certain tantric gods and goddesses have red or blue skin that could be fun to imagine. Some tantric texts describe the body of the lover as translucent or luminous like a rainbow. Think how delightful this could be to envision while stroking your lover's skin!

The tantrikas saw their feelings of passion and desire as having a transcendent aspect, and their mutual attraction as ultimately motivated by a spiritual impulse toward ecstasy. To move in the direction of an attitude like this can help transform the negative messages most of us were brought up with concerning sex. By envisioning our Beloved as divine, it is possible to increase the love in the world and to elevate our ordinary sex acts to acts of worship.

EXERCISE #2:
Do You Want to Tell the Truth?

It may seem scary or daunting to move from a conventional relating style of being positive and not talking about things to tantric relating where you are living in and honoring the truth. It's okay to be where you are in the process—it's more important to tell yourself the truth that you're not ready. First, list the things you're not eager to share with anyone: stories from your past, health concerns, times you screwed up, or politically incorrect feelings such as jealousy, insecurity, and anger.

1.

2.

3.

4.

There also may be things you don't want to hear from your partner. There's an old joke that relates to the differences in the way men and women are socialized: A woman asks her partner to share his feelings, asking him over and over until finally he says, "Okay! I'll tell you how I'm feeling: I feel impotent at work, scared about the future, and I want to have sex with your best friend." "Not that!" yells the woman. "I don't want to hear about that!"

What of your partner's truth would be hard for you to hear?

1.

2.

3.

4.

EXERCISE #3:
Making Agreements

Tantric relating is about making agreements with your partner that you both want to live in an environment of trust, truth, respect, and open communication about what's going on for each of you. It sets completely new ground rules for any relationship.

What tantra offers is not the same as conventional wisdom to smile all the time and hope everything's fine. A lot of people who are working on themselves think it's about being positive no matter what and taking things to a higher level, creating what we call spiritual bypass where people aren't living their truth. They aren't sharing if they're sad, jealous, or upset about what was just said because that wouldn't be upbeat. Resentment builds, and then they are surprised when the relationship starts to tank.

It's a big commitment to make an agreement to talk about everything. It will change your life. If you're not ready at this time, that's okay. Just watch what your results are as you continue on your growth path. You can move slowly toward greater disclosure if that works better for you. One hundred percent commitment, however, is the place where magic begins.

1. Are you ready to make an agreement to talk about everything?

2. When it happens?

3. Until it's done, and the energy is flowing freely again?

4. Are you willing to clear the past? Both your own and the relationship's?

EXERCISE #4:
Clean Sweep

For pure tantric relating you'll need to do a major housecleaning. Anything still bugging you from the past keeps you from being able to be present with what's really happening. An example might be if you grew up with a father who was always criticizing you, you imagine your partner is putting you down when they are not. The past mistreatment has not been resolved, and you're seeing your partner through the eyes of that little person you once were.

This clean sweep can be done in psychotherapy or in any of the other processes mentioned previously. You can also journal, create art about it, or join a therapy or Twelve-step group. Many people are willing and skilled in how to help you with "cleaning out the basement." The sooner you start, the sooner you'll be able to live in the present moment instead of being mired in the past.

Some places I'm still stuck are:

1.

2.

3.

4.

If you're currently in a relationship, the two of you most probably have unresolved issues from the past: arguments that were never resolved, talks about your sex life that need to happen, differences in style in spending habits, child-raising, and future goals. All these matters that need to be settled keep you from being able to have clear, flowing energy between the two of you.

Past issues that we as a couple need to talk through to completion are:

1.

2.

3.

4.

EXERCISE #5:
Raise the Bar

You learned about the Gottman's formula of five statements of praise and gratitude to one correction or request. What if you took this on as a daily discipline to praise, thank, or flirt with your partner five times a day?

There are an unlimited number of things to *praise* about your partner. Here are a few to get you started—circle the ones you want to use and add your own.

- Their hot body
- Their kind heart
- Their competence
- Intelligence
- The way they contribute to you and the family
- Financial independence
- Talents and skills, even little ones
- Good taste in music or movies
- Good values
- Responsibility

It's not hard to *give thanks* to your partner when you recognize their divine nature. Here are a few items to expand on and share:

That you show up for our relationship	Thanks for taking care of your body
That you accept me, warts and all	Picking up after yourself
That you share in the household chores	Accepting my family
For lovemaking	Being an upstanding human being
For talking a walk with me	Being a giver instead of a taker

Figuring out how to *flirt* is really fun. Get creative!

When you're out grocery shopping, pat them on the butt.

Tell them frequently how arousing you find them.

Look in their eyes just a little bit longer and raise your eyebrows and smile.

Buy a silly mug that says something like "World's Greatest Lover."

Order surprise gifts of sexy thongs, especially if their body is unconventionally beautiful.

Remind them of romantic moments from your shared past.

Touch, touch, and more touch.

EXERCISE #6: What Do We Mean by "Spiritual Relationships?"

"WIIFM" is the primary motivator for many people in their relationships. WIIFM is a marketing term for "What's in It for Me?" We have been taught to value people for how good they will look on our arm, how close they come to our fantasy of the ideal lover, or how we imagine they will fulfill our desires. It's about how it all looks, right? Except that when we focus on the outside, nobody is going to be good enough because everyone is flawed. Everybody. This is why we love the tabloids—we get to see seemingly perfect celebrities with their defects hanging out.

One characteristic of a spiritual relationship is that instead of focusing on the other person's exterior, we focus on the perfection within. Just as we all have not-so-beautiful parts on the outside, we all have a perfect core at our center. When we want our relationship to have a spiritual component, we attempt to keep our attention on this perfection within, rather than concentrating on what's outside.

The great tantra master Osho once said regarding relationships, "The Other is always right." I was stunned when I first heard this. Like most people, I had been constantly pointing out when I was right and my partner was wrong, all in the name of "communicating honestly." In retrospect, it was all a thinly disguised power struggle.

I argued with Osho's statement in my mind and then decided to see what I could learn from it. As a technique, I recommend it highly. You don't have to agree with it to experiment. Practice interpreting that the other was right and you were wrong next time you are reviewing a fight or disagreement. The ego spends all its time proving that it is superior. See what happens from the perspective of love.

When you begin this discipline of seeing what is right about the other person rather than what is, according to you, wrong, you may start to experience your partner as your teacher, or guru. Some of the other attributes of spiritual relationships that people have mentioned are placing a high value on listening, integrity, emotional openness, sensitivity, truth, having a raise-the-bar attitude, and having a passion for learning and growing.

When people's lives are dedicated to something higher than just getting their own needs met, their relationships will follow suit. This can show up as a dedication to making the world a better place by working for the environment, helping kids, or serving some other higher calling. Your relationship will be dedicated to something more important than merely trying to get your needs met, and this is what we call a spiritual relationship.

Acknowledgments

Thanks to Radha Luglio, Gitama, Margot Anand, Charles Muir, Carolyn Graham Muir, Sunyata Saraswati, Bodhi Avinasha, Vince Kelvin, Mystery, Osho International Meditation Resort, SkyDancing Tantra, Source School of Tantra, Human Awareness Institute, and Peter Rengel.

Thanks to my readers and collaborators: Sandra Sloss Giedeman, Margaret Drewry Walsh, Lilly Penhall, Ziri Rideaux, Kimberly Grace, Denise Lebre, and Abbe Kantor Jaye.

Thanks to my dream-come-true husband, Greg Lawrence.

Thanks for all the heartbreaks and heartaches, mistakes and missteps, broken fantasies and shattered dreams that were required along the way. They were all worth it to get HERE.

Thanks to the inspiring example set by the following tantric couples. While not all of these people identify as "tantric"—what I mean by the word is that their partnership serves the world and that the spiritual dimension of relationships is acknowledged and lived by them: Diana and Michael Richardson, Alex and Alison Grey, John and Julie Gottman, Peter Rengel and Donna Spitzer, Tom Kenyon and Judi Sion, Sasha and Anne Shulgin, Miten and Deva Premal.

Thanks to the many teachers and systems who teach about the importance of clearing: David Schnarch, PhD, Human Awareness Institute, NLP, Osho Multiversity, The Tech, and Toltec Shamanic Recapitulation.

And most of all on-my-knees gratitude to Osho, the great tantra master.

About the Author

Catherine Auman, LMFT (Licensed Marriage and Family Therapist) is a spiritual psychotherapist and the Director of The Transpersonal Center. She has advanced training in traditional psychology as well as the wisdom traditions. Catherine lived for a year at the Osho ashram in India—a full-time immersion in tantra and meditation—and she has studied and practiced tantra, love, sex, intimacy, and seduction with numerous teachers. She lives in Los Angeles with her husband, Greg Lawrence, with whom she teaches tantra and relationship enhancement.

Connect with Catherine Auman

Websites:	catherineauman.com
	thetranspersonalcenter.com
Facebook:	catherineauman.author
Instagram:	@catherineauman
Youtube:	catherineauman
Eventbrite:	thetranspersonalcenter
Email:	info@catherineauman.com

Works by Catherine Auman

Books

The Tantric Mastery Collection: The Complete Tantric Mastery Series 3-in-1 Compilation
The Tantric Mastery Series (also available in Spanish)
   Tantric Relating: Relationship Advice to Find and Keep Sex, Love and Romance
   Tantric Mating: Using Tantric Secrets to Create a Relationship Full of Sex, Love, and Romance
   Tantric Dating: Bringing Love and Awareness to the Dating Process
Mindful Dating: Bringing Loving Kindness to the Dating Process
Guide to Spiritual L.A.: The Irreverent, the Awake, and the True
Shortcuts to Mindfulness: 100 Ways to Personal and Spiritual Growth
Fill Your Practice with Managed Care

Workshops

Tantra: The Science of Creating Your Soulmate
Tantra: The Foundations of Conscious Touch
Tantric Secrets about Women
Tantric Secrets about Men
Tantra and the Psychedelics of Sex
MDMA and Couples: The Promise of Ecstasy

Audio Recordings

Tantric Embodiment Induction
Deeply Relaxed
Awareness Breathing